Captain James Cook
and the Explorers of the Pacific

General Editor

William H. Goetzmann
Jack S. Blanton, Sr., Chair in History
  University of Texas at Austin

Consulting Editor

Tom D. Crouch
Chairman, Department of Aeronautics
  National Air and Space Museum
  Smithsonian Institution

WORLD EXPLORERS

Captain James Cook
and the Explorers of the Pacific

David Haney

Introductory Essay by Michael Collins

CHELSEA HOUSE PUBLISHERS

New York · Philadelphia

On the cover   Eighteenth-century map of New Zealand; portrait of James Cook

Chelsea House Publishers
Editor-in-Chief   Remmel Nunn
Managing Editor   Karyn Gullen Browne
Copy Chief   Mark Rifkin
Picture Editor   Adrian G. Allen
Art Director   Maria Epes
Assistant Art Director   Noreen Romano
Series Design   Loraine Machlin
Manufacturing Manager   Gerald Levine
Systems Manager   Lindsey Ottman
Production Manager   Joseph Romano
Production Coordinator   Marie Claire Cebrián

World Explorers
Senior Editor   Sean Dolan

Staff for CAPTAIN JAMES COOK AND THE EXPLORERS OF THE PACIFIC
Associate Editor   Terrance Dolan
Copy Editor   Benson D. Simmonds
Editorial Assistant   Martin Mooney
Picture Researcher   Joan Beard
Senior Designer   Basia Niemczyc

First Printing

1   3   5   7   9   8   6   4   2

Library of Congress Cataloging-in-Publication Data

Haney, David.
   Captain James Cook and the explorers of the Pacific/David Haney.
       p.   cm.—(World explorers)
   Includes bibliographical references and index.
   Summary: Examines the life and journeys of Captain Cook.
   ISBN 0-7910-1310-3
         0-7910-1534-3 (pbk.)
   1. Cook, James, 1728–79—Juvenile literature.   2. Explorers—
Great Britain—Biography—Juvenile literature.   3. Pacific Ocean—
Discovery and exploration—Juvenile literature.   [1. Cook, James,
1728–79.   2. Explorers.   3. Pacific Area—Discovery and
exploration.]   I. Title.   II. Series.
G246.C7H327   1991   91-12311
910'.92—dc20   CIP
                                                  AC

CONTENTS

WORLD EXPLORERS

THE EARLY EXPLORERS

THE FIRST GREAT AGE OF DISCOVERY

THE SECOND GREAT AGE OF DISCOVERY

THE THIRD GREAT AGE OF DISCOVERY

CHELSEA HOUSE PUBLISHERS

Into the Unknown

Michael Collins

It is difficult to define most eras in history with any precision, but not so the space age. On October 4, 1957, it burst on us with little warning when the Soviet Union launched *Sputnik*, a 184-pound cannonball that circled the globe once every 96 minutes. Less than 4 years later, the Soviets followed this first primitive satellite with the flight of Yuri Gagarin, a 27-year-old fighter pilot who became the first human to orbit the earth. The Soviet Union's success prompted President John F. Kennedy to decide that the United States should "land a man on the moon and return him safely to earth" before the end of the 1960s. We now had not only a space age but a space race.

I was born in 1930, exactly the right time to allow me to participate in Project Apollo, as the U.S. lunar program came to be known. As a young man growing up, I often found myself too young to do the things I wanted—or suddenly too old, as if someone had turned a switch at midnight. But for Apollo, 1930 was the perfect year to be born, and I was very lucky. In 1966 I enjoyed circling the earth for three days, and in 1969 I flew to the moon and laughed at the sight of the tiny earth, which I could cover with my thumbnail.

How the early explorers would have loved the view from space! With one glance Christopher Columbus could have plotted his course and reassured his crew that the world was indeed round. In 90 minutes Magellan could have looked down at every port of call in the *Victoria*'s three-year circumnavigation of the globe. Given a chance to map their route from orbit, Lewis and Clark could have told President Jefferson that there was no easy Northwest Passage but that a continent of exquisite diversity awaited their scrutiny.

In a physical sense, we have already gone to most places that we can. That is not to say that there are not new adventures awaiting us deep in the sea or on the red plains of Mars, but more important than reaching new places will be understanding those we have already visited. There are vital gaps in our understanding of how our planet works as an ecosystem and how our planet fits into the infinite order of the universe. The next great age may well be the age of assimilation, in which we use microscope and tele-scope to evaluate what we have discovered and put that knowledge to use. The adventure of being first to reach may be replaced by the satisfaction of being first to grasp. Surely that is a form of exploration as vital to our well-being, and perhaps even survival, as the distinction of being the first to explore a specific geographical area.

The explorers whose stories are told in the books of this series did not just sail perilous seas, scale rugged mountains, traverse blistering deserts, dive to the depths of the ocean, or land on the moon. Their voyages and expeditions were journeys of mind as much as of time and distance, through which they—and all of mankind—were able to reach a greater understanding of our universe. That challenge remains, for all of us. The imperative is to see, to understand, to develop knowledge that others can use, to help nurture this planet that sustains us all. Perhaps being born in 1975 will be as lucky for a new generation of explorer as being born in 1930 was for Neil Armstrong, Buzz Aldrin, and Mike Collins.

The Reader's Journey

William H. Goetzmann

This volume is one of a series that takes us with the great explorers of the ages on bold journeys over the oceans and the continents and into outer space. As we travel along with these imaginative and courageous journeyers, we share their adventures and their knowledge. We also get a glimpse of that mysterious and inextinguishable fire that burned in the breast of men such as Magellan and Columbus—the fire that has propelled all those throughout the ages who have been driven to leave behind family and friends for a voyage into the unknown.

No one has ever satisfactorily explained the urge to explore, the drive to go to the "back of beyond." It is certain that it has been present in man almost since he began walking erect and first ventured across the African savannas. Sparks from that same fire fueled the transoceanic explorers of the Ice Age, who led their people across the vast plain that formed a land bridge between Asia and North America, and the astronauts and scientists who determined that man must reach the moon.

Besides an element of adventure, all exploration involves an element of mystery. We must not confuse exploration with discovery. Exploration is a purposeful human activity—a search for something. Discovery may be the end result of that search; it may also be an accident, as when Columbus found a whole new world while searching for the Indies. Often, the explorer may not even realize the full significance of what he has discovered, as was the case with Columbus. Exploration, on the other hand, is the product of a cultural or individual curiosity; it is a unique process that has enabled mankind to know and understand the world's oceans, continents, and polar regions. It is at the heart of scientific thinking. One of its most significant aspects is that it teaches people to ask the right questions; by doing so, it forces us to reevaluate what we think we know and understand. Thus knowledge progresses, and we are driven constantly to a new awareness and appreciation of the universe in all its infinite variety.

The motivation for exploration is not always pure. In his fascination with the new, man often forgets that others have been there before him. For example, the popular notion of the discovery of America overlooks the complex Indian civilizations that had existed there for thousands of years before the arrival of Europeans. Man's desire for conquest, riches, and fame is often linked inextricably with his quest for the unknown, but a story that touches so closely on the human essence must of necessity treat war as well as peace, avarice with generosity, both pride and humility, frailty and greatness. The story of exploration is above all a story of humanity and of man's understanding of his place in the universe.

The WORLD EXPLORERS series has been divided into four sections. The first treats the explorers of the ancient world, the Viking explorers of the 9th through the 11th centuries, and Marco Polo and the medieval explorers. The rest of the series is divided into three great ages of exploration. The first is the era of Columbus and Magellan: the period spanning the 15th and 16th centuries, which saw the discovery and exploration of the New World and the world ocean. The second might be called the age of science and imperialism, the era made possible by the scientific advances of the 17th century, which witnessed the discovery of the world's last two undiscovered continents, Australia and Antarctica, the mapping of all the continents and oceans, and the establishment of colonies all over the world. The third great age refers to the most ambitious quests of the 20th century—the probing of space and of the ocean's depths.

As we reach out into the darkness of outer space and other galaxies, we come to better understand how our ancestors confronted *oecumene,* or the vast earthly unknown. We learn once again the meaning of an unknown 18th-century sea captain's advice to navigators:

> And if by chance you make a landfall on the shores of another sea in a far country inhabited by savages and barbarians, remember you this· the greatest danger and the surest hope lies not with fires and arrows but in the quicksilver hearts of men.

At its core, exploration is a series of moral dramas. But it is these dramas, involving new lands, new people, and exotic ecosystems of staggering beauty, that make the explorers' stories not only moral tales but also some of the greatest adventure stories ever recorded. They represent the process of learning in its most expansive and vivid forms. We see that real life, past and present, transcends even the adventures of the starship *Enterprise.*

Enlightenment and Empire

The famed mariner was not born near the seashore, although it can be said that in England, one is never too far from salt water. The British are islanders, seagoing people, and from their ranks emerged the greatest of the 18th-century nautical explorers—Captain James Cook.

James Cook was born on October 27, 1728, in the rural village of Marton-in-Cleveland, Yorkshire. His father was a Scottish farm laborer, his mother a simple Yorkshire village woman. The Cooks moved to the nearby town of Great Ayton two years after James was born. James spent his childhood there, playing and then working on the farm his father had been hired to manage. Young James had a natural intelligence, which was noticed by a local woman of means, the elderly Mary Walker, who taught him to read. Soon, his potential also came to the attention of his father's employer, who then paid for James to attend the village's one-room school.

James Cook did not stay in school for long. In his midteens he was taken to a small seaport called Staithes, where he was apprenticed to William Sanderson, a grocer and haberdasher. Although he worked in the back of a tiny, dark, and stuffy shop, Cook could hear seagulls calling and smell the salt water, and at night when storms rolled in off the North Sea he would lay awake in bed, listening to the howling winds and the waves pounding the shore. He began pressing Sanderson to allow him to leave his

A portrait of Captain James Cook, painted for the governor of Newfoundland in 1776. The British mariner completed three global voyages from 1768 to 1779, exploring and accurately mapping more of the earth's surface than anyone else before or since.

A cottage with a thatched roof in rural North Yorkshire, England, was the birthplace of James Cook. Cook was born on October 27, 1728. By the age of 18 he was at sea, where he remained, except for brief intervals, for the rest of his life.

service, and eventually Sanderson gave in. Cook immediately made the 12-mile journey to Whitby, a major seaport, and in July 1746 he was apprenticed to the brothers Henry and John Walker, Quakers and coal shippers.

Cook spent most of the next nine years aboard a succession of colliers that hauled coal between Newcastle, London, Norway, and Baltic ports. When he was not at sea he lived in the house of one of his superiors, where he continued to educate himself by studying whatever books he could obtain (mathematics and astronomy were his favorite subjects). The Walkers were impressed with this serious young man, who was eager—and quick—to learn. Cook showed an innate aptitude for sailing, and he was never unnerved by the storms, fogs, hidden shoals, and tricky tides that made the waters off England's east coast notoriously treacherous. He moved steadily up the commercial sailors' hierarchy, from seaman to mate.

In 1755, the Walkers offered Cook command of one of their colliers, which he had undoubtedly earned. But Cook declined the offer. He was tired of lugging coal through the North Sea's gloomy fogs and wintry squalls. He longed to sail new waters and to make new landfalls. So, instead of taking command of the Walkers' ship, Cook joined the Royal Navy. The brothers Walker were quite surprised; Cook would be passing up a chance to command his own vessel in order to join the Royal Navy as a lowly seaman. And the life of the common sailor in the Royal Navy was a hard one; so hard, in fact, that the navy was often forced to resort to impressment to fill its ranks—itinerant or unemployed men, many of them drunks or petty criminals, were arrested by shore patrols and forced to sail on Royal Navy vessels. A British sailor could then look forward to a harsh existence marked by toil, deprivation, war, constant exposure to the elements, and disease.

Nevertheless, on July 25, 1755, with the rank of able seaman, Cook shipped out aboard the Royal Navy's *Eagle*. At that time England was embroiled in a struggle with campaign. In early 1759 it joined a blockade of the Saint Lawrence River designed to prevent French ships from carrying supplies to the fortress-colony of Quebec. Later, British warships entered the Saint Lawrence to attack Quebec, and Cook distinguished himself by successfully navigating the massive *Pembroke* up the narrow, twisting, and frequently shallow waterway. He then participated in the British siege of Quebec.

By 1760, both Quebec and Montreal had fallen to the British, and Cook, now master of the *Northumberland*, had completed a survey of the Saint Lawrence River and had begun charting the coast of Nova Scotia. A London engraver agreed to publish Cook's charts and maps, authoritative geographic surveys that would remain in use for more than a century. By the time of the Peace of Paris in 1763, which concluded the war and made Great Britain master of North America, Cook had firmly established his reputation as a navigator and surveyor of considerable skill. He had also managed to continue his studies and had become proficient in mathematics, astronomy, and navigation.

After his tour of duty in North America, Cook returned home long enough to marry Elizabeth Batts, of the village of Barking. He was 34; she was 21. The couple spent the early part of 1763 together, but after only four months, Cook was commissioned to return to North America to conduct the first survey of the coast of Newfoundland. He spent much of the next five years engaged in this task, returning to England each winter to spend four months with his growing family (the Cooks would have a total of six children, but only three of them survived childhood).

By now, James Cook was the very image of the ideal sea captain. He was tall and strong, with handsome, clean-shaven features and sharp blue eyes, his long hair pulled back from his face and secured behind his head according to the naval officers' fashion of the day. Cook projected an air of resolute competence and quiet authority. A man

In 1759, at the height of the Seven Years' War, British gunships sailed up Canada's Saint Lawrence River and shelled the French colonial city of Quebec. The Quebecois believed that the shallow, narrow river would prevent such an operation, but British navigators—including James Cook—succeeded in getting their ships upriver.

of substantial intellect but few words, he rarely had to raise his voice in order to get things done on a ship—other men seemed to respect him immediately (those who did cross Cook usually regretted it, for he had a ferocious temper). His reputation continued to spread throughout the Royal Navy, Great Britain, and even continental Europe, where leading men of science, as well as the military, were noting with approval the quality and accuracy of Cook's maps and charts. Moreover, powerful forces were at work in Europe. Far-reaching plans were being made, and Cook soon found himself a part of them.

In the 18th century, Europe experienced a period of great intellectual activity known as the Enlightenment. Rational thought, based on scientific inquiry and observation of the natural world, became the guiding principle for the Enlightenment's scientists, writers, philosophers, and scholars. New inventions, such as the microscope and telescope, allowed the curious to explore new inner and outer worlds. All over Europe, scientists were discovering truths about man and his universe and were seeking to apply these truths to the betterment of humanity.

In 1768, the Royal Society, England's premier scientific body and a bastion of Enlightenment thought, convinced the Admiralty to undertake an expedition to the South Pacific to observe the transit of the planet Venus across the sun. A careful observation of this event from various widespread locations would allow astronomers to determine the distance between the earth and sun and also to establish previously unknown longitudes. There were other objectives as well. Both the Royal Society and the British government were hoping that the expedition would clarify the murky, incomplete maps of the South Pacific that current mariners depended upon. Although there had already been substantial exploration of the Pacific, rumor, myth, and wild speculation were still the primary sources of information about that part of the globe.

At the heart of this mythic geography was Terra Australis (Southern Land), a great continent believed to be located somewhere in the South Pacific. For centuries, scientists and cartographers had theorized that there must be a massive continent at the southern end of the globe to "balance" the landmasses of the northern hemisphere. Many believed that the lands of New Zealand and Australia, whose dimensions were largely unknown, were possibly parts of a large continent. It would be the expedition's task, after observing the transit of Venus from the vantage point of the South Pacific island of Tahiti, to sail along the coastlines of Australia and New Zealand in order to determine the shape and extent of these landmasses. The expedition could thus be called a voyage of clarification and enlightenment.

As preparations for the journey began, the Admiralty (the government department responsible for overseeing the navy and maritime affairs) and the Royal Society discussed

A section of James Cook's map of the island of Newfoundland, the Strait of Belle Isle, and Labrador, on the Atlantic coast of Canada, drawn during surveying expeditions he made from 1763 to 1768.

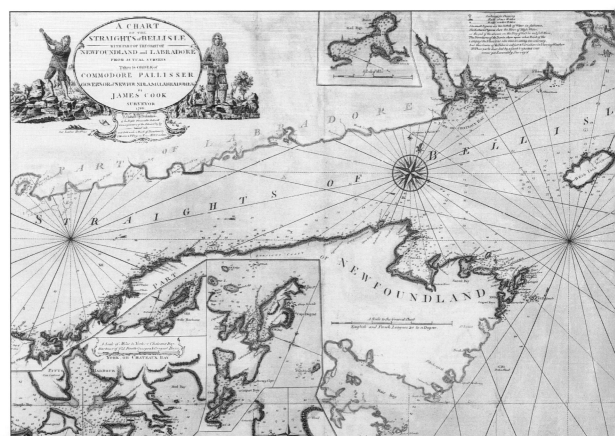

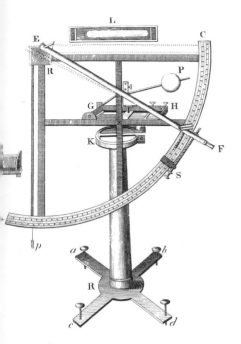

A quadrant of the kind used by navigators in the 18th century. Navigators could determine latitude by using a quadrant to measure the altitude of the sun, the moon, or the North Star. The most accurate nautical quadrants were developed by the Englishman John Bird around 1760; Captain Cook brought one of these on the Endeavour's *voyage.*

possible candidates to lead the expedition. A civilian adventurer, Alexander Dalrymple, was nominated by the Royal Society, but the Admiralty insisted on a Royal Navy officer. Finally, a name was offered that met with the approval of both the scientific and military communities—James Cook.

The Admiralty's insistence on a Royal Navy officer to lead the expedition probably alerted careful observers—including spies working for England's rivals—that the impending voyage was much more than a simple field excursion for the Royal Society. As the recently concluded military struggle between France and England aptly demonstrated, the 18th century was an age of ruthless economic imperialism as well as scientific curiosity. Britain was engaged in a bitter struggle with Spain, France, and Holland for control of the seas and thus for access to new lands and their resources. Cook's voyage, then, was much more than a scientific expedition. He had, in fact, three objectives: to observe the transit of Venus; to settle the confusion over the geography of the South Pacific; and to establish the British Empire's military and economic presence in the South Pacific.

Once Cook had been named captain, preparations for the voyage went swiftly. A ship was chosen. To Cook's satisfaction, the Admiralty picked a 368-ton collier much like the ones he had sailed on during his tenure with the Walker brothers. Although such coal-carrying vessels were sluggish and boxy, the *Endeavour,* as this one was named, would prove perfect for the long, arduous voyage ahead. Colliers were sturdy, built to survive rough seas, and they were large enough to carry a lot of coal or, in this instance, a lot of people and supplies, among other things.

The *Endeavour* would host a complement of 94 people. Because of the multifaceted nature of the expedition, the passengers were an odd mixture for an Admiralty vessel. There were Royal Navy personnel, including officers, common seamen, and a troop of marines. There was a Royal Navy surgeon, and some of the officers brought servants. A one-armed cook was hired. Cook recruited several trusted friends from his commercial-shipping days and others who had sailed on the *Pembroke* or *Northumberland* with him. As Cook knew these men well and had great faith in their abilities, they constituted the core of his crew. He also found a place for his wife's cousin. Finally, there were the Royal Society representatives, or the "experimental gentlemen," as the sailors called them. These included astronomer Charles Green, naturalist Joseph Banks, botanist Daniel Carl Solander and his assistant, and two artists, Alexander Buchan and Sydney Parkinson. The artists were essential, for they would provide a visual record of the expedition in all its natural and geographic aspects.

Cook personally supervised the procurement and storage of supplies. For the transit of Venus, a newly invented, portable observatory was packed away in the ship's hold. Cook also requisitioned every available navigational, mathematical, and astronomical instrument, including some new and as yet unproven devices, which he hoped to test during the voyage. Two reflecting telescopes, a quadrant, two astronomical clocks, a sextant, two thermometers, a surveyor's theodolite, a brass scale, and two proportional compasses were provided by the Admiralty and the Royal Society. Cook's cabin was fitted with a plane table, glass for tracing, and a supply of paper and ink. The importance of these items to Cook was evident—he carried most of them aboard himself, fearing they might be damaged by rough treatment.

Last to be stowed were the edible supplies—enough to feed 94 men for at least 2 years. The *Endeavour*'s hold was stuffed with 34,000 pounds of bread, 10,000 pounds of flour, 120 bushels of wheat, 10,000 pieces of salted meat, 1,500 pounds of sugar, 20 bushels of salt, 2,500 pounds of raisins, 120 gallons of oil, 500 gallons of vinegar, and 1,200 gallons of beer. Large amounts of malt, sauerkraut, and a syrup made from lemons and oranges were packed as well. The Admiralty hoped these last items would prevent scurvy (a disease caused by Vitamin C deficiency), the scourge of sailors for centuries.

Finally, the *Endeavour*, her crew, and her passengers were deemed ready. Cook said farewell to his family and then boarded his ship at the town of Deal, near the mouth of the Thames River. On August 26, 1768, with the winds of enlightenment and empire filling her sails, the *Endeavour* set off for Tahiti.

The Endeavour, *a 368-ton, 106-foot-long collier, sails out of Plymouth Sound in August 1768. Although the ship was broad hulled, slow, and hard to maneuver, it would prove sturdy enough to withstand heavy seas and several close encounters with reefs, icebergs, and submerged rocks.*

Matavai Bay

The *Endeavour*'s first port of call was the island of Madeira off the coast of Africa. It would take about a month to reach the island; in the meantime, the crew and passengers of the ship fell into a daily routine and learned how to go about their business without stepping on each other's toes. While the seamen performed their tasks, Banks dragged a small net alongside the ship, and the artist Parkinson sketched any unusual sea creatures that were caught, after which Banks examined and dissected them. Cook and the astronomer Green spent much of their time testing the new astronomical and navigational instruments and plotting their bearings and course. Cook also took steps to break in his new crew and to establish his authority. The seamen found their captain to be stern but fair, demanding but at the same time understanding, easy to anger but also quick to forgive. They soon understood that above all else, Cook expected the *Endeavour* to remain a clean ship; the captain, well acquainted with the pestilential conditions prevalent aboard most Royal Navy vessels, firmly believed that cleanliness was essential to maintaining the health and morale of his crew.

The *Endeavour* reached Madeira in late September. The expedition stayed there long enough to purchase and load some more supplies, including a live bull and 3,000 gallons of wine. (They also suffered their first casualty at Madeira, when the master's mate, while pulling in the anchor, fell overboard and drowned.) From Madeira they

Matavai Bay, Tahiti, was the original destination of the Endeavour *during Cook's first voyage. The Royal Society believed that it would be an ideal location from which to observe the transit of the planet Venus across the face of the sun, a rare astronomical phenomenon.*

proceeded to Rio de Janeiro, Brazil. According to Cook's journal, during this part of the voyage the *Endeavour* was frequently escorted by "great numbers of porpoises, of a singular species, which were about fifteen feet in length, and of an ash colour."

The ship took on fresh water at Rio de Janeiro and then continued south along the east coast of South America. It reached the southern tip of the continent in December and dropped anchor off Tierra del Fuego, a desolate archipelago separated from the mainland by the Strait of Magellan. Here, in this rocky region, the scientists suffered a tragic misadventure. Going ashore to collect plant specimens, the party became lost. Night fell, temperatures plummeted, and before they could find their way back to the beach, two black servants who had accompanied the scientists ashore collapsed. The others, in danger of freez-

The harbor at Funchal, capital of the island of Madeira, located in the east Atlantic about 440 miles west of Morocco. Cook purchased 3,000 gallons of the island's most famous product—wine—when the Endeavour *stopped there in September 1768.*

ing to death, were forced to leave the servants behind. Hypothermia set in, and the two unfortunate men did not survive the night.

Despite this sobering misfortune, the expedition continued. After rounding Cape Horn, the treacherous southernmost tip of the continent, the *Endeavour* left South America behind and took to the open seas, heading in a relatively straight line northwest toward Tahiti and making good time. While Joseph Banks studied the horizon daily for any sign of Terra Australis, Cook kept a lookout for strong currents or choppy seas, a common indication of a large body of land in the area, but a month passed on the high Pacific without the expedition's encountering any. Banks was disappointed, but Cook, who did not believe in the existence of a great southern continent, was not surprised.

Another month passed before land was sighted. On the morning of April 11, 1769, what appeared to be a mountain rising out of the ocean came into view. This was Tahiti. The island and its inhabitants had been discovered by Europeans just two years before Cook's arrival. Captain Samuel Wallis and the crew of the *Dolphin* had arrived at Tahiti in 1767. Some members of the *Dolphin*'s crew had signed on with the *Endeavour*, and they immediately recognized the mountainous outline of the island. Cook, following Wallis's route, directed the ship around the dangerous coral reefs that surrounded the island until he reached its northern coast. There, a river deposited fresh water into the sea, preventing coral from forming and leaving a gap in the reef large enough for a ship to pass through. Cook brought the *Endeavour* through this opening and dropped anchor in Tahiti's paradisiacal Matavai Bay.

Even from the ship the men could see that the island was breathtakingly beautiful. Black volcanic sand lined the beaches around the bay. Behind the beaches, a dense forest of tropical trees swayed gently in the light ocean breezes.

(continued on page 30)

A page from the ship's log of Captain Cook's first voyage. As with everything else he did, the captain was diligent and precise in keeping the log up to date, although he consistently understated the dangers and hardships that were part of daily life at sea.

Dead Reckoning and Lunar Distances

Captain James Cook was not the first mariner to explore the Pacific Ocean, but he was by far the most important. Sea captains of the 15th, 16th, and 17th centuries had already "discovered" many of the same lands Cook visited, but unlike Cook they could not find these places again. What prevented Cook's predecessors from accurately charting their routes and the locations of their discoveries was their inability to ascertain exactly where they themselves were at any given time.

Sailors had been able to determine latitude (the angular distance north or south from the earth's equator measured through 90 degrees) long before Cook's time. A navigator could establish his latitude by measuring the altitude of the North Star or the sun. First the backstaff (invented by British sea captain John Davis in 1595), then the nautical quadrant, and finally the sextant and octant were used to measure the altitude of a celestial body. But in order to fix the exact location of their ship while at sea, navigators needed to determine longitude (their position on the earth's surface indicated by their distance east or west from the prime meridian of Greenwich, England, and expressed in degrees, minutes, and seconds) as well as latitude.

This was not so easy, however, because the exact time of day was needed to determine longitude and a viable nautical chronometer was not to be perfected until after Cook's final voyage. Well into the 18th century, seamen were still relying on dead reckoning—simply estimating their ship's speed to determine the distance traveled in a certain direction from a given point—to establish approximate longitude, and the results were frequently (and sometimes wildly) inaccurate.

Cook, during his voyages, managed to establish longitude using the lunar distances method, but this was accomplished only with great diffi-culty—it took four men who were proficient in astronomy and mathematics to complete the measurements and calculations needed to determine a longitude. Most mariners, lacking Cook's extraordinary diligence, were unwilling—or unable—to utilize the lunar distances method, which involved the use of sextants to measure angles between the moon and certain stars. But the self-educated Cook mastered the technique in all its complexity and succeeded in teaching it to his officers, and subsequently he returned from his voyages with charts of unprecedented reliability. Thus it was certain that wherever Captain Cook had been, others could go also.

An 18th-century English seaman uses a sextant. In order to measure the altitude of the sun or a star, a sailor would locate the celestial body in the instrument's telescope and move the pivoted index arm (in sailor's left hand) along the curved scale until both the horizon and the sun or star coincided in the telescope. The scale, in the form of one-sixth of a circle, would give the altitude.

(continued from page 27)
Farther inland, the men could see the mountain of Oroh-ena rising from the green canopy of vegetation. The crew was eager to go ashore, having been told by the *Dolphin* veterans of the hospitality of the Tahitians—especially the Tahitian women.

Islanders in canoes paddled out to the ship. The canoes were decked with green tree branches, the islanders' symbol of peace. Cook invited aboard two men who were obviously leaders. The two chiefs, tall, regal gentlemen, joined Cook on deck. Gifts were exchanged; Cook was given Tahitian garments, and he presented his guests with beads and hatchets. In the meantime, other islanders had come aboard and were swarming all over the ship. In their curiosity and excitement, some of them even climbed up into the rigging. Cook watched them nervously until it was apparent that they were quite agile and surefooted.

The chiefs invited Cook ashore. Cook, Solander, Banks, and a troop of marines rowed to the beach and set foot on solid ground for the first time in more than two months. Followed by a huge crowd of Tahitians, the newcomers were given a tour of a village. All the Tahitians seemed friendly and hospitable, and they plied their guests with gifts of food.

Cook and Green spent their first days on the island scouting for an opportune location from which to observe the transit of Venus while Banks and Solander quickly lost themselves in the lush forest, a botanist's Eden of undiscovered flowers and plants. The rest of the crew spent much of the time trading and socializing with the islanders. The Tahitians placed great value on anything made of iron; they traded food such as coconuts, breadfruits, plaintains, and the occasional hog for nails or other iron objects. Cook encouraged this activity, hoping to conserve provisions by using the island's resources to feed the passengers and crew of the *Endeavour*.

From time to time the Tahitians prepared special dinners for their visitors. They used an earth oven in which food was steamed between layers of hot stones and green leaves. One island delicacy, a cooked Tahitian dog, caught the dinner guests by surprise. Most of them politely refused a serving of dog, except for Cook, who was known to eat just about anything. The captain liked the cooked dog and compared it to lamb. (The islanders, for their part, were disgusted by the common sailors' practice of shooting and eating rats.)

Relations between the islanders and the white men were extremely cordial, for the most part. Some members of the crew began to pick up the Tahitian language, and soon many had formed friendships with the islanders. The Tahitian women were especially fond of the white men, and the interaction between the crew of the *Endeavour* and the native women soon took on a decidedly sexual aspect. Although Cook disapproved of this particular form of cultural exchange, he did nothing to stop it except to ban trysts aboard ship.

Naturalist Joseph Banks (seated, with outstretched arms) receives a visit from a delegation of Tahitians, who present him with pigs as a gift. Banks was extremely popular with the Tahitians; he learned their language quickly and spent most of his time among them. "I fear I shall scarce understand my own language when I read it again," he wrote in his journal.

Contact between the islanders and the men of the *Endeavour* did give rise to some problems, however. Not long after the arrival of the expedition, the Tahitians began to manifest troublesome behavior. The islanders were, in the words of Cook, "too much addicted to pilfering." In other words, they stole anything they could get their hands on. Spyglasses, snuffboxes, knives, clothing, and navigational instruments were snatched. Even the Tahitian chiefs engaged in thievery. Many of the objects the Tahitians stole from the newcomers were useless to the islanders, as they had no idea what they were, but this did not prevent the thefts. The white men found such behavior incomprehensible and infuriating, not realizing that this was the Tahitians' way of expressing territoriality, asserting their autonomy, and showing that they were not intimidated by the newcomers.

Inevitably, one of the islanders attempted to steal a musket, and tragedy ensued when the marines opened fire on the young man as he sprinted into the forest with his prize.

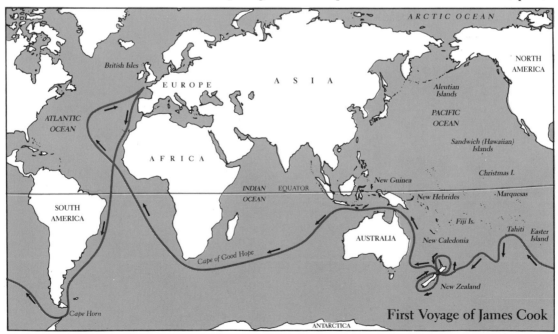

First Voyage of James Cook

The islander was killed and several others were wounded. Civilians Parkinson and Banks were appalled at the shooting. Cook was unhappy about the incident as well, but he also believed that the Tahitians had to be taught that the explorers' firearms were untouchable. The Tahitians, for their part, vanished into the forest for two days. When they reappeared, Cook had little difficulty making peace with them, and soon things were back to normal.

Aside from the problem of theft and the untimely demise of one of the artists, Alexander Buchan, who died after an epileptic seizure, the expedition's business on Tahiti proceeded smoothly. Foremost on Cook's agenda was the observation of the Venus transit, which would occur on June 3, 1769, and he and Green spent much of their time preparing for the event. Cook chose a small peninsula on the north side of Matavai Bay as the site for the observation, and soon the marines began to construct a fort there. A tiny but sturdy stockade was erected; Cook christened it Fort Venus. On either side of the structure lay a bank of earth and a ditch, which prevented anyone from easily approaching it. In addition, Cook had ordered a variety of guns and cannons placed atop the walls. For a final touch, a British flag was hoisted above the miniature castle. The Tahitians were alarmed to see such a thing on their island, but Cook felt the fort was necessary to protect the valuable instruments from the islanders. An astronomical quadrant had already been stolen, and when it was recovered, Green found that the natives had damaged it by attempting to take it apart (fortunately, a member of the crew who had been a watchmaker in London was able to repair it). Cook hoped that Fort Venus would prevent further complications of that sort.

The weather on June 3 was as perfect as Cook and Green could have wished. Not a single cloud could be seen that day, and the air was crystal clear—ideal conditions for observing the celestial event. Cook, Green, and their assistants readied themselves and their instruments, and

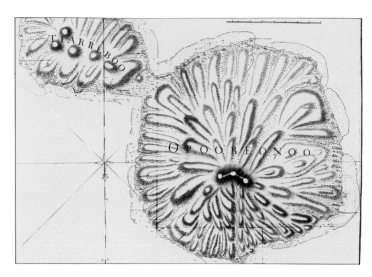

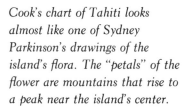

Cook's chart of Tahiti looks almost like one of Sydney Parkinson's drawings of the island's flora. The "petals" of the flower are mountains that rise to a peak near the island's center.

from nine o'clock in the morning to half-past three in the afternoon they watched as Venus moved across the face of the sun. The astronomers were disappointed, however. They had hoped to obtain an exact measurement of the time it took Venus to complete its transit, but because of the planet's penumbra (the halo of light surrounding the planet), they could not determine exactly when Venus itself crossed in front of, and then departed from, the face of the sun. This made an exact timing of the transit impossible, and without an exact timing the observation could only be considered a failure.

The explorers' efforts at ethnography proved more fruitful, as the islanders quickly grew accustomed to the foreigners' presence and allowed them to move about their villages freely. The Tahitians embraced the youthful and engaging Banks in particular—they found Cook to be a bit intimidating—and the naturalist lived in a tent in a Tahitian village, with a Tahitian mistress, for the duration of his visit. In so doing he made himself privy to the less visible elements of Tahitian culture, and he was consequently often called upon to act as a buffer between the members of the expedition and the islanders when the two cultures clashed. For example, when the ship's surgeon was inexplicably beaten by several islanders, Banks prevented any escalation of hostilities by explaining to the surgeon that he had been seen picking a certain flower that was deemed sacred by the Tahitians, and thus had deeply offended the natives by violating their system of taboo, or religious beliefs.

While Banks was involved in ethnographic pursuits, Cook attended to matters of a more geographic and nautical nature. Using one of the *Endeavour*'s launches and enlisting the help of several shipmen, he circumnavigated the island, mapping its coastline. In the meantime, the rest of the crew were engaged in the difficult task of overhauling the *Endeavour*. To gain access to the hull, the ship was heeled, or tilted to one side, in order to expose as much of the hull as possible. With the ship in this position, the men were able to clean the hull and cover it with a protective coat of pitch and brimstone, which would prevent water from seeping into the ship's hold. The crew also inspected the rigging and sails, making repairs where necessary.

After completing his trip around the island, Cook ordered the crew to begin preparations for departure. They had been on Tahiti for more than a month, and friction between the men of the *Endeavour* and the islanders was increasing; the Tahitians continued to steal from their visitors on a daily basis, and they also seemed to be less inclined to provide food. In early July, enmity reached a new level when an iron rake was stolen from Fort Venus. Cook, in retaliation, ordered the confiscation of more than 20 of the islanders' canoes, which he threatened to burn if the rake was not returned. The issue was settled peaceably, but Cook and the islanders were clearly running out of patience with each other. It was time to go.

Fort Venus was dismantled, and the *Endeavour* was readied for departure. The sailors said their good-byes and exchanged gifts and souvenirs with the islanders. Many of the shipmen were given permanent souvenirs—tattoos.

The Tahitians were expert practitioners of the art, and most of them had elaborate tattoos themselves. Upon returning to England and Europe, Cook's men proudly displayed their tattoos, thus initiating a seaman's tradition that still exists.

Some members of the ship's crew were not as eager as Cook to take leave of the fair island; two of them disappeared before the captain had a chance to raise anchor. The two marines had apparently fallen in love with a

couple of island women and had decided to stay. Cook would not have this. Search parties were sent into the islands' interior. The islanders attempted to shelter the star-crossed lovers, but they were apprehended and returned to the ship nevertheless. On July 13, the *Endeavour* passed out of Matavai Bay. Banks expressed sorrow at leaving his many Tahitian friends, and the two would-be deserters wept bitterly, but Cook was glad to quit the island and take to the open sea once again.

The body of a Tahitian chief, attended by a servant, lies in state. The islanders believed that in the afterlife members of their ruling class went to a better "heaven" than did ordinary citizens when they died.

"The Leak Now Decreaseth"

When the *Endeavour* sailed out of Matavai Bay in August 1769 it carried an additional two passengers: Tupaia, a Tahitian priest, and his servant, Tayeto. Tupaia, an inquisitive and intelligent man, had requested permission to join the expedition. Cook was reluctant at first; he wondered how the priest and his servant would react to life aboard the ship and he could not guarantee that the Tahitians would ever be returned to their home. But Banks, who wanted to bring the islanders back to England, argued in favor of Tupaia, and when the Tahitian claimed to know the way to other islands west of Tahiti, Cook granted him and his servant permission to come along.

True to his word, Tupaia directed the *Endeavour* to an archipelago of tiny islands west of Tahiti. With Tupaia navigating, the *Endeavour* sailed from island to island for three weeks (the Tahitian not only navigated with skill and precision but occasionally used his powers as a holy man to summon benevolent winds). Tupaia knew the names of all of the islands, including Raïatéa, his birthplace. Cook claimed all the islands for Great Britain, naming them the Society Islands in honor of the Royal Society. Then, following the orders given to him by the Admiralty, Cook turned the *Endeavour* to the southwest and took to the open sea in search of the great lost continent.

Many dreary weeks on the Pacific ensued. A month passed with no sign of land. Tupaia asserted that there was no great continent in the South Pacific, but only Cook

An elaborately tattooed Maori warrior. (Note the comb, earring, and frog pendant.) Cook first encountered Maoris on the North Island of New Zealand about four months after leaving Tahiti. He soon learned that the native New Zealanders were of a more warlike disposition than were the Tahitians.

believed him. The monotony was unrelieved. Despite the grumbling of the crew, the captain steadfastly enforced his nutritional and hygienic regulations: The men were required to bathe once a day and to fumigate their quarters and clothing once a week. They were also required to eat a certain amount of fresh, vitamin-rich food—such as sauerkraut, raisins, and lemon and orange juice—instead of salted meat, in order to ward off scurvy. Cook was serious about this; two sailors who refused their rations were flogged. Although the men complained (they hated the sauerkraut), Cook's policy seemed to be paying off, for the crew had remained remarkably free of disease to that point.

September came and went with still no sign of land. Cook began to sail in a zigzag pattern, alternately northwest and southwest. The crew began to wonder if there was any land at all out here; each morning they awoke and came on deck to see the horizons undisturbed in every direction. The only actual information Cook had about a landmass at these latitudes was more than a century old. In 1642 a Dutch mariner named Abel Tasman, exploring the southeast coast of Australia (where he discovered the island of Tasmania), was blown eastward for hundreds of miles by strong winds. One morning an extensive, mountainous coastline was sighted. Tasman dispatched a shore party. These men were attacked by hostile inhabitants and forced to retreat to their ship after four of them were slain. An indignant Tasman named the place where his men were assaulted Murderers' Bay and then sailed on to discover the Tonga and Fiji islands. There was much speculation about the mysterious landfall of Abel Tasman. Perhaps he had stumbled upon Terra Australis? Dutch authorities gave the place a name—New Zealand—but made no more attempts to locate or explore it.

Finally, in early October, after 2 months and 1,500 miles at sea, land was sighted. One of the youngest members of the crew, who happened to be named Nicholas

Young, made the sighting from his perch on the masthead. In his honor, Cook named the part of the island that had first come into view—a rocky promontory—Young Nick's Head. As they drew closer, the east coast of the North Island of New Zealand became visible. It looked to be a formidable landmass, with heavily wooded mountains looming behind a rough coastline. Virtually the entire crew concluded that they had found the lost continent, but Cook was unconvinced.

The inhabitants of New Zealand were no more happy to see Europeans coming ashore than their ancestors had been a century before. The aboriginal New Zealanders, known as Maoris, immediately showed their displeasure at encountering the unexpected visitors, behaving in a distinctly inhospitable manner and breaking into *haka*, a wild, frightening form of dancing. Subsequent attempts on the part of Cook to establish relations with the Maoris ended in violent confrontations, and several Maoris were shot and killed. Cook, like Abel Tasman before him, decided it was best to move on. He named the inlet where they anchored Poverty Bay, "because it afforded us no one thing we needed," and sailed on.

Cook headed south along the coast, then turned the *Endeavour* around and sailed north, occasionally stopping and sending men ashore. On November 9 he dropped anchor long enough for Green to observe the transit of Mercury; Cook named this place Mercury Bay. Banks and Solander frequently ventured ashore and found a profusion of animals, plants, and flowers unheard of by European scientists. Parkinson sketched frantically throughout, trying to record the exotic new specimens of plants, the coastline itself, and the Maoris. The artist was fascinated by the elaborate tattoos the Maoris displayed, and he did his best to capture them on canvas. The native New Zealanders, for their part, were alternately friendly and hostile. At some places, such as Tolega Bay, the Maoris traded peacefully with the *Endeavour*; at other locations, such as the aptly named Cape Runaway, the explorers were forced to flee for their lives from huge canoes full of angry Maori warriors. (The men of the *Endeavour* were astonished at the size of the Maori battle canoes, which could hold up to 100 warriors.)

The *Endeavour* rounded the northernmost tip of New Zealand in late November and then sailed down the west

coast. From the ship, Banks and Solander observed a land-scape of dunes and scrub grass. Unlike the lush east coast, it was barren and dry and apparently had little to offer. As he negotiated the unknown coastline, Cook had to remain constantly on the lookout for reefs or shoals that might damage the *Endeavour*. In late December the ship struck a submerged rock and began leaking slightly. Cook

A Maori war canoe could carry as many as 100 warriors. At New Zealand's Mercury Bay one of these canoes circled the Endeavour *for hours as the Maoris studied the alien ship, which they had at first thought was a gigantic seabird at rest on the water.*

searched for a place to stop and repair his vessel. On January 14, the *Endeavour* arrived at a broad, deep inlet that Cook named Queen Charlotte Sound. Cook eased the ship into a cove on the southern side of the inlet. This was a perfect location for the overhauling of the ship; there was plenty of timber and fresh water available here. Cook, apparently feeling uninspired at the time, named the place Ship Cove. Repairs began and reconnaissance parties were sent out. To their alarm, they discovered that the beach was strewn with the bones and skulls of humans. The local Maoris, who seemed quite friendly, informed the visitors that these were the remains of their enemies, whom they had eaten. Most of the sailors were horrified by the idea of cannibalism, but Banks was intrigued and even purchased the preserved head of a victim to bring back to England.

The argument over the alleged southern continent continued. Cook was by now convinced that New Zealand was not attached to any large landmass, and the local inhabitants had informed him that New Zealand was actually two islands separated by a strait. In late January, Cook and a sailor climbed a hill in hopes of viewing Queen Charlotte Sound in its entirety. Looking to the east, Cook discovered that what he and everyone else on the *Endeavour* had supposed to be a bay or inlet was in fact neither of these. Instead, it was the mouth of a strait that apparently connected the seas on either side of New Zealand.

On February 7, 1770, Cook guided the *Endeavour* into this channel (known today as Cook Strait) and followed it eastward between New Zealand's North and South islands. After a fast, unnerving passage through the narrow channel, the ship emerged on the eastern coast. Cook immediately sailed north, up the coast, and completed a full circumnavigation of the North Island. He then reversed his course and began a long, clockwise circumnavigation of the South Island. The crew marveled at the wild, green, mountainous landscape of the South Island, but Cook was

reluctant to interrupt the voyage at this point, and there were few opportunities to go ashore. The *Endeavour* arrived back in Queen Charlotte Sound without mishap on March 24, 1770. Cook and his crew had achieved a remarkable feat for their time, circumnavigating both of New Zealand's islands and thus proving conclusively that they were not part of another landmass. Cook had also charted and mapped in detail virtually every mile of New Zealand coastline. His maps of New Zealand proved to be so accurate that they would remain the standard for years to come.

The *Endeavour* had now been at sea for two years, and Cook began to plan the journey homeward to England. In order to continue his exploration of the South Pacific, he chose a western rather than an eastern route. He decided to return by way of Australia and the East Indies,

Once Banks had gained their confidence, the Maoris of Queen Charlotte Sound, where the Endeavour *anchored for repairs in early 1770, were friendly and helpful, informing Cook that the sound was actually the mouth of a waterway (known today as Cook Strait) that split New Zealand into two separate islands.*

Among the animals encountered off the coast of Australia was the elephant seal, Mirounga angustirotris. *The largest of all the seals, mature* Mirounga *bulls can grow to 20 feet in length and weigh as much as 5,000 pounds, and their "trunk" produces a deep roar. The elephant seal is now an endangered species.*

eventually crossing the Indian Ocean and rounding Africa's Cape of Good Hope to reach the Atlantic. On March 31, Cook pointed the *Endeavour*'s prow toward the setting sun and made for the coast of Australia.

Australia's west coast had been briefly visited by a few European explorers over the past two centuries, but the east coast, known in those days as New Holland (Dutch explorer Abel Tasman had named it from afar in 1644) was for the most part unknown. On April 29, 1770, the *Endeavour* dropped anchor in a bay on the east coast, near present-day Sydney. A landing party went ashore to find fresh water; its members sighted a few naked inhabitants armed with long spears and streaked with white paint. Others paddled about in primitive canoes and were ap-

parently so busy fishing that they hardly seemed to notice the arrival of the white men. Finally, two of them came down to the beach to confront the strangers but were scared off when the marines fired their guns.

The area around the bay was then explored. A variety of terrain was encountered, including sandy, prairielike expanses, swamps, forestland, and, farther inland, rich meadowlands, which Cook, perhaps remembering his boyhood days on the farm, noted would be ideal for grazing sheep (as indeed it would prove to be in years to come). Parkinson sketched as much of the landscape as he could while Banks and Solander discovered a plethora of new plant specimens. Banks was so excited with these findings that a new name was given to the bay. At first, Cook had called it Stingray Harbor because of the large numbers of stingrays inhabiting it (stingray steak was the crew's staple diet during their stay). Now its name was changed to Botany Bay.

The *Endeavour* left Botany Bay after a week and continued north, up the coast. Cook, in his dogged way, charted the coastline mile by mile. The crew glimpsed plumes of smoke rising from the mainland, which suggested that the native inhabitants might be warning one another of the presence of the strange craft off the coast. Cook anchored again on May 23 in a large open bay fed by a stream of fresh water. He named this inlet Bustard Bay, because of the profusion of bustards (large game birds) there.

With a new supply of fresh water, Cook continued northward, still hugging the Australian coast. On a calm, clear moonlit night in early June, the *Endeavour* sailed to the landward side of the Great Barrier Reef, the 1,250-mile stretch of jagged coral that runs along the northern half of Australia's east coast. The narrow seaway between the Great Barrier Reef and the coast is a mariner's nightmare, a treacherous gauntlet of abrupt shoals, freak tides, and submerged coral outcroppings that can disembowel a ship. Not long after the *Endeavour* entered this channel the reef seemed to close in upon the ship, and one of the most harrowing episodes of the voyage began.

Cook eased the ship through these waters slowly and carefully. The crew recognized the danger and performed their duties in virtual silence as the creaking vessel slipped between sandbars, small islands, and coral protrusions. Cook ordered continuous soundings and thus managed to keep the ship in deep water. Gradually, it appeared that the immediate danger had passed; soundings were consistently deep and the sea ahead seemed undisturbed. The crew relaxed. Exhausted from the tension, most of the men turned in. Cook retired to his cabin. Not long after, the *Endeavour* slammed into the reef.

As soon as he came on deck Cook knew that his vessel was in serious trouble. The *Endeavour* was caught on the reef, and looking over the side of the ship the captain could see pieces of wood from the hull in the water. Seawater was flowing into the hold, and the ship was being pounded against the reef by the waves. In an attempt to get the *Endeavour* off the reef, the crew jettisoned all nonessential cargo. Several crew members descended into the watery hold and worked the ship's pumps furiously. Cook's crew performed gallantly in this desperate time, and there was absolutely no panic—there was "not even an oath" to be heard from them, Banks recalled with admiration—although they all knew that the *Endeavour*'s lifeboats had nowhere near the capacity to carry all the passengers. Cook, still in his nightshirt, feared that the leak in the hull would prove to be too much for the sailors manning the pumps, but they held their own. Finally, the incoming tide floated the ship free of the reef.

But as the ship moved off the reef more water began to pour through the hole in the hull and the pumps could not keep up with the influx. The *Endeavour*, Cook realized, was sinking. Everyone began to think about the multitude of sharks they had seen cruising the reef. At this

(continued on page 57)

The Observers

The mariner and his charts, a portrait by Nathaniel Dance.

The wide variety of cargo and personnel that could be found aboard the *Endeavour*, the *Discovery*, the *Adventure*, and the *Resolution* was a testament to the changes in the nature of exploration that were occurring in the 18th century. Although colonial-imperial ambition was the driving force behind expeditions such as Cook's, the acquisition of knowledge was beginning to assume a new importance, and thus pure science was well represented, in the form of both men and instruments, on Cook's ships. *Observation* was the most important word in the vocabulary of the 18th-century scientist, and therefore the artists who sailed with Cook—most notably William Hodges and John Webber—were indispensable, for only they could actually reproduce what was observed. But Webber, Hodges, and their fellow artists were never satisfied with using their talents to simply record— they were *artists*, after all—and whenever they could, they brought their own personal vision into play. The result, as seen on the following pages, was a rich combination of the artistic and the empirical.

The Endeavour *caught in an afternoon squall off the coast of New Zealand, by William Hodges.*

The Resolution *and the* Adventure *anchored in a Tahitian bay, by William Hodges.*

A native New Zealander, by John Webber.

Queen Charlotte Sound and inhabitants, New Zealand, by John Webber.

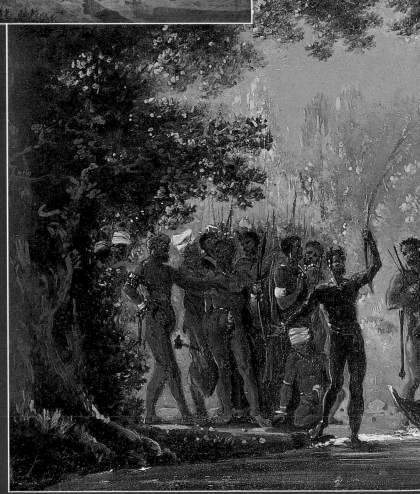

Captain Cook's landing in the New Hebrides, by William Hodges.

The death of Captain Cook, Kealakekua Bay,
Hawaii. Many English artists were inspired
to paint Cook's death by Webber's famous
eyewitness portrayal, which may be seen at
the end of this book.

(continued from page 48)

point a midshipman named Jonathan Monkhouse had an inspiration; he suggested they make an attempt at *fothering* the leak. Fothering was a crude and all-but-forgotten process. Cook described it in his journal: "We mix oakum [twisted fiber impregnated with tar, extracted from the ship's ropes] and wool together and chop it up small and stick it loosely by handfulls all over a sail and throw over it sheeps' dung [there were sheep onboard] or other filth. The sail thus prepared is hauld under the Ship's bottom by ropes . . . While the sail is under the Ship the oakum etc. is washed off and carried along with the water into the leak and in part stops up the hole."

To the relief of everyone, the fothering worked. "The leak now decreaseth," Cook wrote gratefully in his journal. The *Endeavour* limped into a nearby bay and dropped anchor; it took seven weeks for the repairs to be completed.

After its near-disastrous encounter with the Great Barrier Reef, the Endeavour *is heeled (tipped to one side to expose the hull) for repairs. The ship's carpenters discovered that a large chunk of coral from the reef had lodged in the hole in the hull, thus preventing the ship from sinking immediately.*

In the meantime, everybody enjoyed a steady diet of fresh food, and the surrounding countryside was explored. One of the men was out hunting one day when he caught a glimpse of what appeared to be the biggest rabbit he had ever seen, hopping along at an incredible speed and cov-

ering astounding distances with each hop. It was as big as he was, he assured his shipmates, who laughed at him. But several other sightings of the strange creature were reported, and when the local aboriginies were questioned, they informed the visitors that what they had seen was

During Cook's survey of Australia's east coast, the men of the Endeavour *encountered many animals they had never before seen or heard of. Many different kinds of birds and wildfowl were sighted, including the kiwi (lower right, with long, pointed bill) and the emu (top right). In addition to kangaroos, shore parties also sighted extraordinary mammals such as the Tasmanian wolf (striped animal on the left), the platypus (second from bottom on the left), and the echidna (above platypus).*

known as a kangaroo. Soon one of the men shot one, and Banks was able to examine the fantastic animal, after which it was cooked and eaten.

The *Endeavour* set sail again in early August. One would think that after the near disaster on the Barrier Reef, Cook might stear clear of it and continue up the coast well outside the reef. But Cook was determined to chart the coastline and for this he needed to be close. Thus, the next few weeks were nerve-racking, a sore trial for the passengers and crew, who nevertheless recognized what a marvelous bit of seamanship they were witnessing. The captain himself spent a lot of time up on the masthead scouting the reef, and several times the *Endeavour* narrowly escaped disaster. Cook was equal to the task, however, and in late August the ship rounded Cape York, leaving behind the east coast of Australia—which Cook named New South Wales and formally claimed for Great Britain—and the Great Barrier Reef.

Cook now intended to discover whether Australia was linked to New Guinea, another point of contention between 18th-century explorers and cartographers. If it were not, Cook logically assumed that there would be a strait between them that would allow him to continue westward. There was indeed such a channel, known today as Torres Strait, and Cook took the *Endeavour* through despite more reefs and rough seas. The last leg of the marathon voyage was now underway, and everyone aboard the *Endeavour* looked forward to its completion.

In early October the *Endeavour* put in at Batavia (present-day Djakarta), a seaport on the island of Java in Dutch Indonesia. Here, while the ship was overhauled yet again, the passengers enjoyed the company of fellow Europeans for the first time in more than two years. Captain Cook had gone to great lengths to insure the health of his crew and passengers, and his efforts had been rewarded with unprecedented success. Not a single member of his crew had died of disease, an almost unheard of occurrence for

After three relatively healthy years at sea, Captain Cook was faced with the grim reality of tropical disease when he put in at the Indian Ocean port of Batavia, on the island of Java. When the Endeavour _left Java, it carried two new passengers— malaria and dysentery—and Cook could only watch helplessly as the expedition was decimated._

a voyage of that duration. But Cook's precautions against scurvy could not protect everyone from the diseases that flourished in dank, humid Batavia, and before the _Endeavour_ could be overhauled and resupplied for the home stretch across the Atlantic, malaria and dysentery were ravaging the passengers and crew. The men who had survived more than two years of hazardous exploration in the South Pacific now died one after another. Cook got away from the malarial island as fast as he could, but by the time the _Endeavour_ rounded Africa's Cape of Good Hope in March 1771, 33 lives had been lost. Green, Parkinson, Tupaia and his servant, the ship's surgeon, and midshipman Monkhouse, the hero of the Barrier Reef episode, were among the dead. It was a grim ending to what had been, in most respects, an exemplary voyage of discovery.

Resolution and Adventure

On July 12, 1771, the *Endeavour* sailed up the Thames River. It had been almost exactly three years since the men had last seen England. Cook went immediately to his house in Stepney to see his family. The other survivors of the odyssey bid farewell to their shipmates and dispersed in all directions, happy to be home and, after the horrors of Batavia, happy to be alive.

The return of the *Endeavour* was greeted with fanfare and sensational stories in the British press. Banks and Solander attracted most of the public's attention; both men had large collections of "curiosities" to display, including insect and plant specimens they had gathered (not to mention the preserved head of a cannibal's victim), and soon both had become celebrities and were being feted nightly at London's finer addresses. Cook, on the other hand, was virtually ignored by the press and the public, which was fine with him, for he was unconcerned with that kind of recognition and preferred to spend time with his wife and children.

Cook's first official duty upon returning to England was to report to the Admiralty and to the Royal Society. He wrote two detailed reports—one for the Royal Society that primarily concerned the transit of Venus and one for the Admiralty secretary concerning the performance of the navigational instruments he had used during the voyage and his success in preventing scurvy. Cook then reported in person to Lord Sandwich, first lord of the Admiralty,

King George III of England paid Captain Cook the honor of congratulating him personally for the success of his first voyage. Cook had expanded George's empire into the far reaches of the South Pacific, providing the king, who was losing his grasp on his North American colonies, with the possibility of new frontiers.

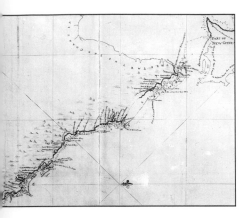

Unlike most of the explorers who preceded him to the South Pacific, Captain Cook returned from his expeditions with concrete information about the area, including detailed and accurate charts and maps such as this one of Australia's east coast.

to discuss the geographic aspects of his voyage and their implications. He was also given an audience with the king.

Cook's superiors were immensely pleased with the captain's performance. He had accurately charted nearly 5,000 miles of coastline, including the entire circumference of New Zealand and the whole east coast of Australia. He had proved conclusively that there was no great continent anywhere between Cape Horn and Tahiti or in the vicinity of New Zealand, Australia, or New Guinea. (Australia is indeed a continent, but what believers in Terra Australis were expecting was a landmass comparable in size to Eurasia and the Americas; on that score, Australia did not qualify as the great unknown southern land.) And, to the everlasting approval of King George III, Lord Sandwich, and the Admiralty, he had established a firm foothold in the South Pacific for the British Empire.

Cook provided members of the Admiralty and the Royal Society with descriptions of the various lands he had visited and the inhabitants he had encountered, and he offered his thoughts on potential colonization. He felt that New Zealand, and especially the North Island, was ripe for colonization. New Zealand's abundant timber, seafood, and edible vegetation could, he contended, not only sustain British settlers but also supply them with "many of the luxuries of life." Cook had also found on the North Island a type of broad-bladed grass that could be used to make rope, and he speculated that the iron-rich sand of Mercury Bay was an indication that New Zealand possessed large quantities of iron ore. From the patterns of native settlement, Cook surmised that the North Island would be the best choice for colonization. The Maoris lived almost entirely on the North Island, and unlike the inhabitants of the more sparsely populated South Island, they seemed to be thriving.

Despite the huge distances Cook had covered during the voyage of the *Endeavour*—more nautical mileage than any explorer or mariner up to that point—he had seen but a small portion of the entire global Pacific Ocean. The Admiralty still believed that the great southern continent was out there somewhere in that immense expanse of water, and Cook was not home for two months before plans for a second expedition, to be led by him, were being made. Cook himself had already envisioned an expedition that would put the Terra Australis question to rest once and for all, and now he addressed his proposal to the Admiralty.

Cook proposed that a second expedition enter the Pacific by way of the Cape of Good Hope rather than Cape Horn. He also recommended that two ships be sent this time, in order to guard against the kind of disaster that would have occurred if the *Endeavour* had gone down off the coast of Australia. Such was the Admiralty's confidence in Cook that it readily accepted these proposals and any other advice he offered as preparations for the second voyage got under way. The *Endeavour* had held up very well during its three-year circumnavigation, and Cook wanted two similar vessels—colliers—for the second expedition. The Admiralty purchased 2 colliers, the *Resolution*, with the capacity to hold 112 people, and the smaller *Adventure*, which could carry 81. Cook would command the former, and Tobias Furneaux, a well-regarded veteran of Samuel Wallis's expedition to the South Pacific, would captain the latter.

Cook hoped to man the two ships with as many veterans of the first expedition as possible. He needed as many of these proven, experienced officers and seamen as he could get, and he succeeded in recruiting a number of them despite their memories of Batavia. There were many newcomers as well; the youngest were 13-year-old midshipman John Elliot and 14-year-old able seaman George Vancouver (who would go on to become a noted explorer in his own right). Unlike the Royal Navy, the scientific community would be sending all new representatives. Two astronomers—William Wales and William Bayley—were

A portrait of Captain Cook. The Admiralty, the king, and the Royal Society recognized James Cook as the man most responsible for the expedition's success, although the public was more interested in the colorful naturalist Joseph Banks. When a second survey of the South Pacific was planned, Cook was the first and only choice for captain.

chosen by the British Board of Longitude. The board,
which was still trying to determine an accurate method of
establishing longitude at sea, also supplied Cook with a
new type of azimuth compass and four new nautical chro-
nometers to test. A new artist, William Hodges, was hired.
Joseph Banks and Daniel Solander would not be a part of
the expedition because of a disagreement with the Admiralty. A well-known German scientist, Johann Forster,
would serve as a replacement. Forster, with Cook's permission, brought his 18-year-old son along with him.

Cook wanted his ships to be fully provisioned, and he
got pretty much anything he asked for. Indeed, so much
material was loaded onto the two vessels that some of it
had to be removed for safety reasons. When Cook was not
personally overseeing the outfitting of the *Resolution* and
the *Adventure*, he was working out the details of his route
with the Admiralty. It was agreed that Cook should sail
around Africa's Cape of Good Hope, explore the waters
south of the cape and then sail eastward across the Indian
Ocean to New Zealand. From there, he would simply
head due south until he ran into a continent or satisfied
himself that there was no large landmass in that part of
the Pacific. If he did indeed find land, he was to explore
and map it in as much detail as he possibly could. If, on
the other hand, he found no continent, he was to continue
east and circle the world, keeping his ships as far south as
was practicable. Cook was instructed to take possession of
any new islands he encountered, and on the return to
England secrecy was to be strictly enforced in order to
prevent England's rivals—particularly France—from taking advantage of or credit for English discoveries.

In July 1772 the *Resolution* and the *Adventure* sailed
out of Plymouth Sound and made for the Cape of Good
Hope. Cook intended to begin his second round of nautical
explorations by searching the waters south of the cape in
order to verify or discount an alleged discovery made by

a French explorer in 1739. The Frenchman, Lozier Bouvet, had been looking for a place called France Australe— yet another mythical continent. A 16th-century French explorer had supposedly seen this landmass, and Bouvet also claimed to have glimpsed it through heavy fog about 1,500 miles south of the Cape of Good Hope. Bouvet named his "discovery" Cape Circumcision, after the Christian feast day on which he sighted it. Cook believed in France Australe about as much as he believed in Terra Australis, but he wanted to eliminate any lingering doubts about such places.

The *Resolution* and the *Adventure* reached Madeira in August. There, Cook purchased voluminous amounts of onions and wine for the voyage. At other ports on the way to the cape, he procured quantities of pigs, goats, fowl, fresh fruits, and water. In late August the crowded ships were drenched by heavy rains, but otherwise their passage to the cape was uneventful. The two ships reached the Cape of Good Hope in late October. The explorers stayed in South Africa for a month, resting, eating as much fresh food as possible, and enjoying the hospitality of the Dutch governor. The Forsters became friends with a young Swedish naturalist who was living on the cape, Anders Sparrman, and prevailed upon Cook to allow the young Swede to join the expedition. Finally, in late November, the *Resolution* and the *Adventure* left the Cape of Good Hope behind. With Cook's ship leading the way, they sailed southward, toward the Antarctic.

The Cape of Good Hope, at the southern tip of Africa, was reached by the Resolution *and the* Adventure *in October 1772. After a month's stay, Cook led the expedition due south into unknown waters.*

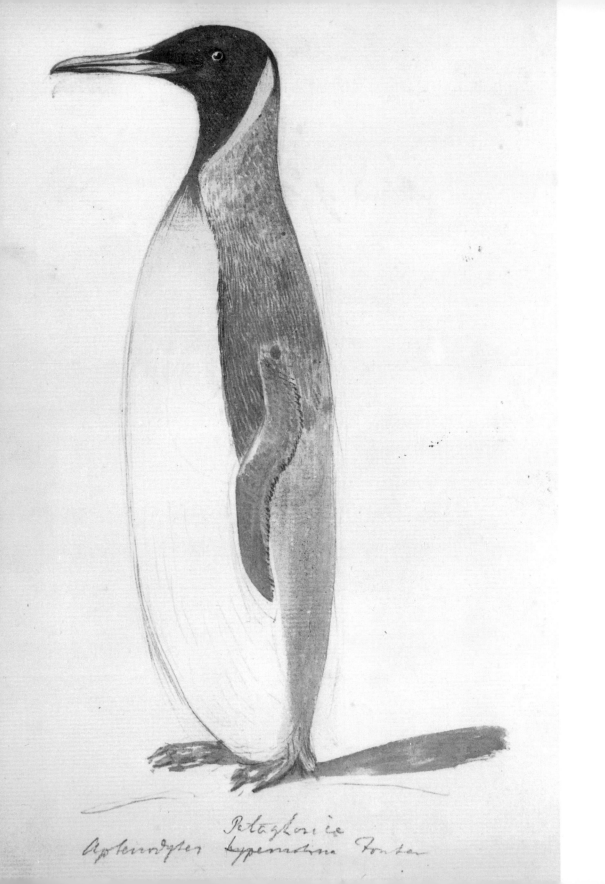

Patagonica

Aptenodytes patagonica Forster

"I Have Never Seen So Much Ice"

None of the men on the *Resolution* or the *Adventure*, no matter what their background, were prepared for the hardships that awaited them as they sailed toward the bottom of the world. As Cook began his search for Bouvet's Cape Circumcision and the ships entered the higher latitudes of the southern Atlantic waters, the temperature dropped steadily, the seas became rough, and gale-force winds began to rip at the masts and sails of the colliers. In these unforgiving seas all hands gained a new appreciation for the sturdy if unlovely build of the two coal-hauling vessels. Lighter, faster, more streamlined ships could not have survived extended periods in such waters.

As the ships pressed southward the temperature continued to drop. Week-long gales prevented either vessel from raising its sails. The seas were monstrous and waves frequently swept the decks. The animals aboard died in large numbers. And although the crew was issued extra clothing, life on deck was brutal. Everything was covered with ice—including the seamen themselves. Snow and sleet pelted the ships continually, and sometimes the fog was so thick that the men could not see well enough to complete their duties. Cook was his usual self, however—these waters reminded him of his youthful days on the North Sea—and despite the miserable conditions the men remained healthy and morale was high.

On December 11 the explorers encountered a gigantic pyramid of ice. According to the elder Forster it was twice

Cook's second expedition was marked by two grueling forays into Antarctic waters. Determined to go as far south as he possibly could, Cook pushed his crew and ships to the limit. As they sailed among the icebergs, the men frequently amused themselves by counting penguins, which were plentiful in that region.

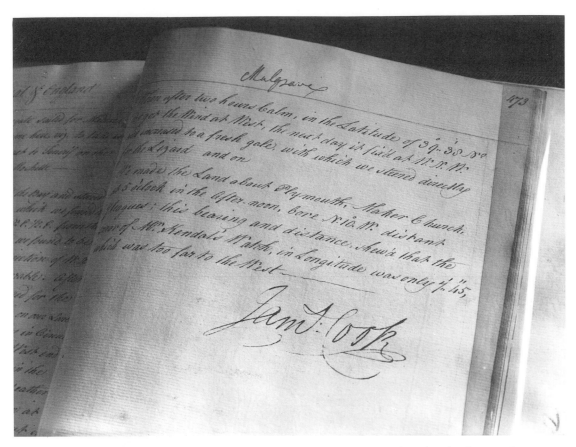

No matter what the conditions or circumstances, Cook kept the ship's log up to date, recording not only practical information but his thoughts and impressions. Of the gigantic icebergs that menaced his ship, Cook wrote that the sight of them "at once fills the mind with admiration and horror, the first occasioned by the beautifullniss of the Picture and the latter by the danger attending it."

as tall as the *Resolution*'s masthead, which was about 200 feet high. At first the men believed they had sighted land, but as they drew closer they saw that it was actually a huge, free-floating chunk of ice, or what they called an ice island. Everybody congregated on deck to have a look at this marvel. They encountered more and progressively larger ice islands as they moved southward, along with heavy fog and temperatures well below freezing. The two colliers were now in truly perilous seas, and even the veterans of the *Endeavour*'s brush with the Great Barrier Reef were unnerved.

Cook and his officers were constantly on deck now, as were the captain and officers of the *Adventure*. The fog was impenetrable, but it seemed to have an amplifying effect on sounds. The cries of strange animals came to them out of the mist, and from all directions appalling creakings and great, thunderous splashings could be heard—the sounds of monumental objects colliding or scraping against one another. Monstrous icebergs would materialize suddenly out of the thick fog, frighteningly close to the ships, and occasionally the mist would clear long enough for those on deck to see that they were sailing through waters that were crowded with these floating mountains of ice. Gathered at the railings, the men watched in awed silence as the mammoth icebergs slid by, knowing that to even brush against one of them meant, in the words of one officer, "nothing but immeadate Death."

Cook pushed southward and Furneaux followed. The fog cleared as the temperature continued to plummet. Now they encountered cracked fields of ice that stretched to the east, west, and south as far as the eye could see. Despite the apparently harsh environment, there was abundant wildlife. The men saw seals, whales, penguins, and various other birds. Cook was now navigating his ship through narrow channels in the ice pack and Furneaux was doing his best to follow. The captain of the *Adventure* could occasionally be seen shaking his head in silent amazement—or perhaps horror—as Cook inched through a particularly tight squeeze. On December 15 the ships were stopped by a sheer wall of ice. The *Resolution* and the *Adventure* were virtually surrounded by ice at this point; worried about being trapped, Cook—to the relief of everyone on both vessels—decided to retreat.

The ships went north until they had cleared the ice, then turned east, dropping anchor on Christmas Day for a party. After this brief respite they continued eastward. On New Year's Day they reached the alleged location of Cape Circumcision but could see no sign of land whatsoever, and Cook concluded that Bouvet had probably mistaken an iceberg for land. The captain turned to the

south again, and soon the ships were in the midst of the
ice. In mid-January 1773, the expedition became the first
in the history of nautical exploration to cross the Antarctic
Circle; no ship had ever sailed so far south. An enormous
ice field prevented the ships from continuing any farther;
Cook directed them northeast, then southeast, all the
while searching for any sign of a continent. On February
8, during a gale, the ships became separated. The plan
under such circumstances was for the *Resolution* and the

Adventure to rendezvous at New Zealand, so Cook stayed on an eastward course until mid-March, then turned to the northeast and headed directly for New Zealand. The *Resolution* arrived in New Zealand's Dusky Sound near the end of the month. Cook and his crew had been at sea for 117 days and had sailed 10,980 nautical miles. Only one member of the crew was sick.

Dusky Sound, located on New Zealand's southwest coast, proved to be an ideal place for the sea-weary men

Cook's ships probe for a safe channel through the ice pack. From December 1772 to February 1773, the Resolution, *followed by Captain Furneaux's* Adventure, *pushed southward through ever-thickening ice. In January 1773, Cook's ships became the first to cross the Antarctic Circle; soon after, the two vessels were separated in a storm.*

of the *Resolution* to rest. Almost everyone, including those who had sailed on the *Endeavour*, agreed that Dusky Sound was the most beautiful spot they had ever visited, a natural enclosure of coves and lagoons, streams and rivers, and pools and shallows, protected on three sides by towering cliffs. The cliffs were heavily wooded, and waterfalls replenished the pools at their base. The bay was shielded from direct sunlight for most of the day, and a fine mist was always present, as if a wispy cloud had taken a liking to the spot and settled there permanently. The overall atmosphere was shadowy, quiet, and restful, and there was plenty of cool clear water to drink and fresh fish and wildfowl to eat. Dusky Sound was so obviously beneficial to the health and spirits of the crew that Cook decided to stay there for longer than he had originally planned.

After seven weeks, the *Resolution* sailed out of Dusky Sound with a well-rested complement of scientists, officers, marines, and sailors. Cook made for Queen Charlotte Sound, where he hoped to rendezvous with Captain Furneaux. On May 18, the *Resolution* sailed into Queen Charlotte Sound and the men were greeted with the welcome sight of the safely anchored *Adventure*. Furneaux had been waiting for Cook for six weeks; after becoming separated from the *Resolution*, Furneaux had sailed for New Zealand. The captain of the *Adventure* assumed that both parties would now spend the southern winter at New Zealand, but Cook had had quite enough vacationing and he informed Furneaux that they would be sailing northward to the tropics for the winter, after which they would return to New Zealand in time to reprovision the ships and make another Antarctic excursion in the summer.

In early June 1773 the *Resolution* and the *Adventure* sailed out of Cook Strait and headed east and then north. They reached Matavai Bay in mid-August, having seen absolutely no sign of land since New Zealand. The Tahitians remembered the *Endeavour*'s visit, and they eagerly crowded onto the new ships. The expedition spent two weeks at Tahiti. Those who had been aboard the *Endeavour* renewed old acquaintances while the newcomers explored the island and got to know the Tahitians. There were the usual problems with petty theft, but for the most part relations between the Tahitians and their visitors were as friendly as usual.

After Tahiti, the ships visited some of the smaller islands of the Society chain. At Huahiné, the voyagers bought nearly 400 hogs, as well as other delicacies, from the islanders. The hogs were slaughtered, cooked, salted, and stowed away for leaner times at sea. A young Huahinian man joined the crew of the *Adventure* when it embarked. His name was Mai but his shipmates dubbed him Jack (the Huahinians, for their part, called Captain Cook "Cookee"). Mai would eventually make it to England, where he would become something of a celebrity. At Raïatéa, the islanders robbed the visitors with great ingenuity. They also treated Cook and his men to a dramatic performance, which included, appropriately, the enactment of a robbery.

The expedition continued in a southwesterly direction. In October it reached Tonga, discovered originally back in 1642 by the ubiquitous Abel Tasman. The Tongans were friendly and hospitable. Their chief entertained a party of the visitors at his house, a neat rectangular building with fenced-in gardens and a well-kept lawn. A group of Tongan girls sang for the guests; Cook returned the gesture by having the ship's bagpipe players perform, which pleased his hosts greatly. The inhabitants of the other islands in the area proved equally hospitable, and Cook named the entire group the Friendly Islands.

The *Resolution* and the *Adventure* were back at their New Zealand base by the end of October. Cruising off the coast of the North Island, the ships were overtaken by a heavy storm that continued for a week. When the storm lifted, the men on the *Resolution* saw that their sister ship was gone. Cook proceeded to Queen Charlotte Sound, hoping the *Adventure* would show up there. Anchored in Ship Cove, the *Endeavour*'s former resting place, the *Resolution* was overhauled and prepared for another Antarctic voyage while Cook kept an impatient lookout for the other ship. November came and went but there was still no sign of the *Adventure*. Cook could wait no longer. He wrote a message to Furneaux, put it in a bottle, and buried it beneath a tree near the beach, which was marked with the words *Look Underneath*. Then the *Resolution* sailed down Cook Strait into the Pacific and headed due south.

By mid-December the *Resolution* was once again at high latitudes. These were the most grueling weeks of any of Cook's expeditions. If anyone had forgotten the hardships of the previous Antarctic voyage they received a bitter reeducation now. It was a time of clammy fogs that enshrouded the ship for days, of driving sleet and snow, of rolling swells and bitter cold. But mostly, it was a time of ice. The ship, as it approached the Antarctic Circle once

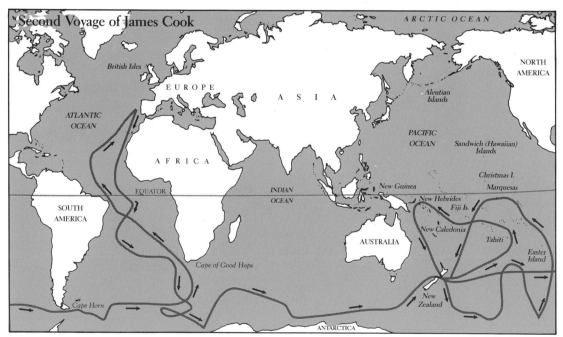

again, had become entirely encrusted with ice. Every inch of the vessel, below and above decks, was layered with ice, including the officers' cabins and the crew's quarters (and their beards). There was nowhere to go to escape the dampness, the cold, the ice. Cook described the weather and the vessel's condition in the ship's log for Friday, December 24: "Wind northerly, a strong gale attended with thick fogg, sleet and Snow, which froze to the Rigging as it fell and decorated the whole Ship with icicles. Our ropes were like wire, our sails like plates of metal, the sheaves froze fast in the blocks. I have never seen so much ice."

Cook coaxed and bullied his ship as far south as the ice would allow; when the pack ice finally stopped him he sailed north out of the ice fields, then east, and then he plunged to the south a second time, only to be repulsed by the ice once more. There was an almost obsessive quality to Cook's behavior during this part of the voyage; the idea of sailing to the south yet again was horrifying to everyone aboard except for him. The officers and crew were frozen, exhausted, and depressed, and the civilian passengers were openly expressing their dismay. Nevertheless, in the final week of January, Cook gave the order to head south, and the ship crossed the Antarctic Circle for the third time. Still Cook was not satisfied. Finally, on the frigid morning of January 30, a wall of ice was sighted, stretching unbroken as far as the men could see in both directions. To the south were towering mountains of ice, "rising one above another till they were lost in the Clouds." Cook had clearly gone as far south as he could, coming closer to the South Pole than any explorer before him. (In that part of the Antarctic no ship has ever gone farther south.) Grudgingly—"I will not say it was impossible anywhere to get in among this ice," he later wrote— Cook gave the order to turn northward.

The *Resolution* had covered a huge swath of the Pacific since leaving New Zealand. Cook had successfully eliminated any remaining doubts about the possible existence

Three views of Easter Island. A tiny speck of land in the vast Pacific, Easter Island lies 2,000 miles off the coast of Chile. Exhausted from their second Antarctic ordeal, Cook and his men anchored off the island in March 1774.

of a large continent in the waters between the Society Islands to the north and the Antarctic to the south, New Zealand to the west and Cape Horn to the east. He was satisfied that if any continent existed in the frozen nether reaches of the world, it had to lie so far south as to be virtually unreachable through the ice.

Most of the crew believed—and hoped—that they would now sail for home. They were disappointed, but they probably should have known better, most of them having been at sea with Cook for at least two years. Cook informed them that they would be sailing north and then west again, and that there was as yet a solid year of exploration ahead of them. The captain's plan was to sail north for Easter Island, discovered in 1722 by Dutch explorer Jacob Roggeveen. The exact location of Easter Island was uncertain, and Cook hoped to find and chart the island. From Easter Island he would proceed northwest to the little known Marquesas, then southwest to the Society Islands, due west to the New Hebrides (present-day Vanuatu) and south to New Caledonia, eventually arriving yet again at New Zealand, where the *Resolution* could be overhauled and reprovisioned for the voyage to England.

Easter Island was sighted in mid-March, to the delight of everybody, for they had not seen land in three months. It was a small, nondescript island inhabited by Polynesians much like the natives of the other South Pacific islands Cook had visited. The most notable feature of Easter Island was the massive ancient statues, carved from volcanic rock, that were scattered all along the coast, some leaning this way or that, some fallen to the ground, all with their inscrutable stone faces looking out to sea. The statues were—and still are, to a certain extent—an anthropological mystery. It seemed clear that the ancestors of the island's current inhabitants could not have had the engineering skill to transport and erect such monoliths; the stone faces were all at least 20 feet high, and some of them weighed as much as 50 tons. As Cook mused in his jour-

nal, "We could not help wondering how they were set up, indeed if the Island was once Inhabited by a race of Giants." The islanders themselves had no significant information about the statues, and Cook and the others could only speculate on their origin.

After five days on Easter Island, during which Cook and the ship's astronomer fixed the island's exact coordinates, the *Resolution* headed northwest, toward Tahiti. About 900 miles northeast of the Society Islands, Cook made a detour to the north, hoping to find a group of islands discovered in 1595 by a Spanish expedition. The Spaniards had named the island group the Marquesas, after the governor of Peru. The Spanish expedition's navigator, Pedro de Quiros, returned to the area several years later but failed to find the islands again. In early April 1774 one of Cook's men spotted an island, and thus the *Resolution* became the first European vessel to visit the Marquesas in almost two centuries.

The people of the Marquesas proved to be quite advanced compared to most of the other island peoples Cook was familiar with. Their houses were well made and rested upon stone foundations, and their canoes, though small, were also finely constructed. They carried clubs and spears of good craftsmanship, yet they were as friendly as any islanders the expedition had yet encountered. The men were tattooed "from head to foot," Cook recorded in his journal. Their language resembled that of the Tahitians, which allowed the visitors to establish trade relations with them rather easily. Nevertheless, another incident of theft led to the death of a young Marquesan, which cast an ugly shadow over the explorers' visit.

Three days after leaving the Marquesas the *Resolution* was once again anchored in Matavai Bay. Cook, as always, enjoyed a warm reception on Tahiti. In fact, the islanders were so hospitable and food was so plentiful that Cook extended his stay to six weeks. The crew used the time to refit the ship and stock it with fresh supplies, which the islanders gladly exchanged for red feathers that the explorers had obtained at Tonga. Cook noted that the feathers were "as valuable here as Jewels are in Europe." The inevitable conflict over theft arose; some Tahitians robbed a hunting party, taking everything the hunters carried— even their clothes. Cook seemed to be growing tired of these episodes, for he had one of the islanders flogged for stealing a small water cask.

After Tahiti, Cook visited some of the neighboring islands, including Oparre and Mooréa, which were about to go to war with one another, and Raïatéa. In early June the *Resolution* put in briefly at Niue, one of the Friendly Islands. Cook gave this supposedly friendly island a new name—Savage Island—after one of its inhabitants hurled a spear at him. From Niue the crew could see the glow of a volcano on the neighboring island of Tofua, which lit the night sky.

In mid-July, Cook reached the New Hebrides, an island group originally discovered by the Spanish navigator Quiros. Cook carefully charted the group and obtained the islands' native names from the inhabitants, who were constantly rowing alongside the *Resolution* in their canoes. Another volcano, on the island of Tana, rumbled ominously and showered the decks of the ship with ashes. Cook visited Eromanga and Tana but did not stay long because of confrontations with the islanders. After a brief stay at Espíritu Santo, the northernmost of the New Hebrides, he set sail for New Zealand.

In early September, the *Resolution* arrived at the island of New Caledonia, which lies to the north of New Zealand. There, the people proved friendlier than those at recent landfalls and showed no inclination to steal from their visitors, something which immediately and permanently endeared them to the voyagers. New Caledonia was well planted and carefully watered. Since the islanders possessed no domesticated animals of any sort, Cook left them a boar and a sow to get them started. He also delighted a local chief by giving him a pair of puppies.

The *Resolution* arrived at Queen Charlotte Sound in mid-October. There, Cook discovered that the bottle containing the message for Furneaux was gone, and there were signs that trees had been cut and an observatory constructed. The islanders confirmed that the *Adventure* had in fact visited the area and had stayed two or three weeks. Cook was relieved that the ship was apparently safe. Now preparations for the voyage home began. Everyone, including Cook, was deeply homesick, and they were ready to go by early November. Cook intended to head straight for South America, cutting across his route of the preceding summer in case he had missed any undiscovered lands in that region. On November 11, 1774, the *Resolution* passed out of Cook Strait and sailed due east for Cape Horn.

A landing party from the Resolution was turned back by the inhabitants of Eromanga, one of the New Hebrides Islands, when it attempted to go ashore there in July 1774. Two of Cook's men and four islanders were wounded in the skirmish.

"As Fair a Prospect as I Can Wish"

The *Resolution* sailed into Plymouth Harbor on Saturday, July 29, 1775. The ship had been at sea for 3 years and had covered 70,000 miles of ocean. Cook's second voyage is now recognized as one of the greatest—if not the greatest—nautical journeys of exploration ever undertaken. His exhaustive reconnaissance of the South Pacific proved once and for all that there was no great landmass there aside from Australia; it also proved that with proper diet and living conditions long-duration voyages could be accomplished with minimal risk of disease. (Only four men died on Cook's second voyage, and none from scurvy.) But if Cook or anyone else on the *Resolution* expected a hero's welcome upon returning to England they were disappointed; their return was largely ignored by the press and the public. The primary reason for this was the return of the *Adventure*; Furneaux had brought his ship back to England a year before Cook and had, in effect, stolen Cook's thunder, for there were some rather sensational aspects of the *Adventure*'s voyage that had caught the public's fancy.

One of the first things Cook did upon returning to London was to find Furneaux; Cook was as eager as anyone else to know what had happened to the *Resolution*'s sister

Mai of the Society Islands was brought to England aboard the Adventure, *which arrived a year before Cook and the* Resolution *returned. The young Polynesian created quite a stir. Although his hosts initially expected him to behave like a savage, they quickly found that Mai was, in the words of one observer, "decent" and that "his deportment is genteel, and resembles so much that of well bred people here."*

England's prestigious Royal Society, which had for so long benefited from the endeavors of Captain Cook, rewarded him upon his return from the second voyage by making him a fellow, or member, of the society.

ship and its crew. It was, Cook soon learned, a grim tale. Furneaux informed Cook that after becoming separated from the *Resolution* off New Zealand the *Adventure* had been driven far out to sea by the storm. Once the storm lifted, Furneaux, according to the prearranged plan, sailed to Queen Charlotte Sound. Furneaux arrived at the sound just days after an impatient Cook had embarked on the second Antarctic excursion. While the *Adventure* was anchored, Furneaux sent a party of 10 men ashore to gather supplies. The men never returned. Furneaux sent a second party ashore to look for them. These men found the longboat their comrades had used; it was empty except for several pair of shoes. Moving inland, the search party surprised a group of Maoris, who appeared to be eating a meal. When the New Zealanders saw the marines they ran off, leaving the remnants of their meal and several baskets behind. The baskets were filled with the flesh of the 10 missing sailors, who had been killed, cooked, and partially eaten by the Maoris. Horrified, the marines fled back to the ship and informed the captain of their grisly discovery. Furneaux decided to sail for England.

The story of the Massacre at Grass Cove, as it was called, drew a lot of attention, sold a lot of British newspapers, and, even a year later, overshadowed Cook's accomplishments. Cook did not care about the lack of publicity, but he was puzzled by the massacre itself. Cook, unlike most of his countrymen, was unconcerned with the cannibalism; he knew that the Maoris did not kill humans to eat them but rather ate of their vanquished enemies as a ritual celebration of victory in battle. It was the murder of the sailors that troubled him. Cook had spent a substantial amount of time dealing with the Maoris and although they could be fierce when they felt threatened, they were for the most part civil and friendly. In Cook's own words, the New Zealanders were "Brave, Noble, Open and benevolent." But they were also "a people that will never put up with an insult." Cook concluded that the sailors must have provoked the New Zealanders in some way, but he would not learn the truth of the matter until he returned to New Zealand.

Along with the story of the Grass Cove incident, Furneaux brought Mai of Raïatéa back to England with him. Mai was a hit in London, a living curiosity, an exotic, tattooed "savage" from the South Pacific. Joseph Banks immediately took the young Polynesian in hand and paraded him through the drawing rooms of London, where Mai was poked, prodded, gawked at, and generally looked down upon by his hosts. The Raïatéan proved to be remarkably adaptable, however, and in a short period of time he mastered European manners and made many friends in England.

Although the general public did not at first give Cook the acclaim he deserved for his second voyage, the people who most counted to the captain did. He was given an official presentation at the court of King George not long after his return to England, and the Admiralty promoted him to the high rank of post-captain. Perhaps most gratifying to Cook was his admittance to the Royal Society in early 1776—a great honor and a substantial achievement for a person who was almost entirely self-educated. And for his work toward the prevention of scurvy, Cook was awarded the Society's Copley Medal, given each year to an individual who had made essential contributions to science.

Cook was now 47 years old. He intended to stay on land long enough for him to spend time with his wife and his children—whom he hardly knew—and to prepare for publication a written account of his second voyage. In order to establish a sufficient income he accepted a prestigious administrative position at Greenwich Naval Hospital. But Cook had always been a restless man, incapable of remaining in one place for too long, and within months he was yearning to return to the seas. "Months ago the whole Southern hemisphere was hardly big enough for

Cook accepted a lucrative position at Greenwich Naval Hospital in the summer of 1775. Although he admitted that the job represented "a fine retreat and pretty income," it was not long before the captain's restless nature reasserted itself.

In February 1776, Lord Sandwich, first lord of the Admiralty, put an end to Cook's retirement by offering the captain command of a third Pacific expedition. Cook, who was 47 at the time, hesitated only briefly before accepting.

me," he wrote to a friend in the summer of 1775, "and now I am confined within the limits of Greenwich Hospital, which are far too small for an active mind like mine."

It did not take the Admiralty long to make another offer to Cook. In February, Cook's good friend and patron, Lord Sandwich, invited the captain to dinner and offered him command of another Pacific expedition. Cook seemed uncertain at first but by the time dessert was served he had accepted. It was a fateful decision on the part of the captain. "It is certain I have quited an easy retirement, for an active, and perhaps Dangerous Voyage," he explained to a friend, "but my present disposition is more favourable to the latter than the former, and I embark on as fair a prospect as I can wish."

Cook's first two voyages had been exercises in geographic reality; their most important result was the destruction of myth. Fittingly, for his third voyage Cook was charged with the task of either finding or discounting one of the most tenacious of geographic chimeras—the Northwest Passage, the long sought after, navigable seaway that supposedly linked the Atlantic and the Pacific via Canada's Arctic waters. Such a passage would provide a quick route to the Orient for European shipping, eliminating the long, dangerous trips around the capes of Africa or South America.

The hunt for the Northwest Passage had been underway for centuries. British explorers Martin Frobisher and John Davis had searched the east coast of North America for the passage in the 16th century, and Dutchman Henry Hudson expanded upon their efforts until 1610, when his crew mutinied and set him adrift. Though he was never heard from again, his discovery of Hudson Strait raised hopes that the passage in fact existed. In 1612, British navigator Sir Thomas Button sailed through Hudson Strait, proving that it was not part of the passage. Other expeditions since then had failed to locate the Northwest Passage.

For the third voyage, Cook planned to follow the route of the second voyage, around the Cape of Good Hope and across the Indian Ocean, first to New Zealand and then to the Society Islands to return Mai to his homeland. From there Cook would sail due north to North America's west coast, where the search for the passage and a general reconnaissance of that region would begin. Cook was given two ships; he would captain the trusty *Resolution* once again, and, because the *Adventure* was unavailable, the Admiralty purchased another ship, the *Discovery*, as the second vessel. The Admiralty gave the command of the *Discovery* to Charles Clerke, who had sailed with Cook aboard the *Endeavour* and the *Resolution*.

Most of Cook's tried and true veterans from the first two voyages would accompany him on this third and last venture. There were new men as well. The new master of the *Resolution* was a hot-tempered 22-year-old named William Bligh; he would become infamous in his later years as captain of the mutinous *Bounty*. A new second lieutenant, James King, would also be the astronomer for the *Resolution*. David Samwell would be the new surgeon's mate on the *Resolution*; Samwell would write a detailed account of the voyage and would eventually become a poet of some renown. John Webber, a landscape painter, was the new artist.

Cook's third expedition sailed from England on July 12, 1776. The weather was fair and a stiff wind was blowing as the *Resolution* and the *Discovery* cleared the English Channel. All hands were on deck to bid a final good-bye to their home waters, and spirits were high as the ships took to the open sea. Some of Cook's officers, however, noticed that the captain seemed unusually quiet and preoccupied as he looked out to sea. Years later, after the fateful voyage was over, these officers could not help but remember James Cook's demeanor on that day, and they could not help but wonder if their captain had experienced some premonition or foreshadowing of things to come.

Resolution and Discovery

On the passage to the Cape of Good Hope, the *Resolution* began to show signs that the years at sea were taking their toll. The seams of the ship had not been adequately caulked during the latest layover at the dockyard, and soon the men could hardly get out of bed without their feet becoming soaked. Cook, whose temper would grow increasingly volatile as the voyage progressed, was irate, but understandably so in this instance. The porous seams were but the first in a series of structural problems that would arise, and the *Resolution* would require constant maintenance throughout the expedition.

In October, both ships reached Table Bay, in present-day South Africa. There, the *Resolution* was caulked again and the expedition procured two years' worth of provisions in addition to the cows, horses, goats, and sheep they had carried from England. (Cook intended to seed some of the South Pacific islands with these animals in the hope that they would flourish there and provide a new food resource for the native inhabitants and also for future visitors, including European colonists.) Thus, the two vessels were quite crowded when they sailed from Africa at the end of November, and in a letter to the Admiralty, Cook joked, "Nothing is wanting but a few females of our own species to make the *Resolution* a complete ark."

Cook headed southeast in order to investigate a French discovery in the southern Indian Ocean, the island of Kerguelen. The island proved barren and inhospitable,

A woman of Unalaska, painted by John Webber, the Resolution's *official artist for Cook's third expedition, in June 1778. Unalaska is one of the Aleutian Islands, located off the southwest coast of Alaska. The Unalaskans, according to one of Cook's officers, were "to the last Degree obliging and civil, as intrinsically so, as any degree whatever of civilization could render them."*

and at the end of December the expedition sailed for New Zealand. The new year brought dense fogs, squalls, and rough seas. The ships eventually reached Tasmania, south of Australia, and anchored in Adventure Bay. After a brief stay they proceeded to New Zealand, anchoring in familiar Queen Charlotte Sound on February 12.

The local Maoris, even those who were known personally by members of the expedition, would not approach to trade or socialize, believing that Cook had come to punish them for the Grass Cove incident. The captain had no such intention, especially after he went to the site of the massacre to investigate the episode and learned from witnesses and some of the Maoris involved that, as he had suspected, a fight had developed when several of the marines overreacted to the theft of some food and opened fire on a group of islanders. Although Cook assured the islanders that he was not there to exact vengeance, relations between the Maoris and the visitors never quite recovered. Many of the members of the expedition, knowing that the

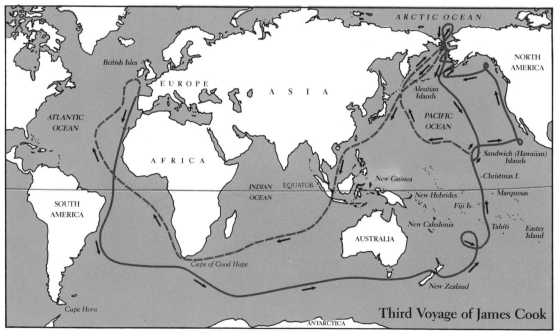

Third Voyage of James Cook

islanders had made a picnic out of a number of their fellow Englishmen, could not help but regard the Maoris with repugnance, and the islanders remained wary. There were no sad farewells on either side when the ships sailed out of Queen Charlotte Sound in March.

Cook's destination was now the Society Islands, but because of unfavorable winds the expedition was forced to make a detour eastward to the Tonga Islands. Before they reached the Tonga group, they discovered the tiny islands of Mangaia and Atiu, part of a small archipelago that would come to be known as the Cook Islands. The *Resolution* and the *Discovery* reached the Tonga Islands on April 30. They stayed until the middle of July, spending most of their visit on Tongatapu, the largest of the Tongas, as guests of Paulaho, one of the more powerful chiefs of the islands. Trade with the natives proved fruitful, and some of the livestock was brought ashore and the islanders were introduced to animal husbandry.

But before long, relations between the islanders and the visitors became strained. Theft, as always, was an irritant, and on Tongatapu, Captain Cook began to react to the islanders' mischievous behavior with an unusual—for him—lack of tolerance. Previously, Cook had always viewed this aspect of the Polynesians' behavior with an anthropological detachment. If something of real value was stolen he would simply send some men to take it back, and if the perpetrator refused to return the object in question Cook would confiscate property (usually canoes) and hold it until the stolen item was returned. At worst, the captain would ask an influential islander to come aboard his ship and remain there as a kind of token hostage until the islanders returned the stolen goods.

Now, however, Cook began to resort to corporal punishment. He had an islander flogged for theft. When the stealing continued, Cook himself shot and wounded an islander, and he ordered that a cross be carved into the arm of another as punishment for throwing a stone at a

A man of Mangaia, an engraving from a drawing done by Webber in April 1777. Mangaia is one of the Cook Islands, located southwest of the Society Islands. The inhabitants of Mangaia were fierce; they planned to kill Captain Cook and his men if they got a chance, but Cook, recognizing their hostile intentions, did not allow anyone to go ashore.

marine. Subsequently, by the time the expedition left Tongatapu, tensions were high. This disturbing trend continued at the Society Islands, where the expedition arrived in mid-August to return Mai. There, Cook had the heads of islanders shaved as a punishment for stealing, and when some of the expedition's goats disappeared, the captain had the marines march on several villages, where canoes were destroyed, houses were put to the torch, and hogs were shot. But instead of intimidating the Polynesians, Cook succeeded only in provoking them and stoking their growing resentment of the foreigners. The situation escalated, and by the time the ships left the Society Islands behind in December, Cook, despite the protests of many of his officers, had gone to the grotesque extreme of having offending islanders' ears lopped off.

Cook's behavior toward the islanders during his third voyage should be viewed as the symptom of an ailment the captain was suffering from rather than some kind of

Hawaiian islanders put on a fighting exhibition for their guests in December 1778, during the second visit of the Resolution *and the* Discovery. *Cook's expedition had first discovered the Hawaiian Islands a year earlier, during its voyage from the Society Islands to North America.*

moral deterioration or character flaw. Cook was not himself during this period; relations with his crew and passengers were unusually strained during the third voyage, and his temper, always notoriously short, was more explosive than ever. Clearly something was out of order with the captain; something other than the islanders' by now familiar behavior was bothering him. Cook biographer Lynne Withey suggests that the captain was suffering from a severe vitamin deficiency—the result of a digestive ailment that had troubled him during much of the second voyage. The symptoms of a vitamin deficiency of this kind can include depression, irritability, anger, and even paranoia. Whatever the case, it seems that Cook may have driven himself too hard; like the leaky *Resolution*, he was showing the effects of many hard years at sea.

From the Society Islands, the two ships sailed due north. On Christmas Eve, 1777, a tiny, lonely island was sighted in the vast, uncharted waters of the North Pacific. The Englishmen named it Christmas Island and stopped long enough for some of the crew to catch 300 of the large sea turtles that swarmed in the waters offshore. The decks of both ships were crawling with turtles as they continued northward, and turtle meat was part of the regular diet for some time to come.

On January 18, 1778, 3,000 miles northwest of Tahiti, in a part of the Pacific where the word *mainland* has no meaning, Cook came upon a scattered archipelago—the Hawaiian Islands. (Cook named them the Sandwich Islands after Lord Sandwich.) He cruised among these islands until, off the island of Kauai, he found a safe anchorage, a rare occurrence here, where the coastlines lay open to huge rolling waves. Going ashore, Cook and his companions were surprised to find that the local inhabitants were Polynesians much like the occupants of the islands of the South Pacific. "How shall we account for this nation spreading itself so far over this vast ocean?" Cook mused in his journal. The Hawaiians had obviously never seen white men before; many of them seemed to think Cook was a god, and, to the captain's horror, they hurled themselves to the ground and hid their face whenever he passed by. But they also engaged in a brisk trade with the newcomers and were never so awestruck by Cook that they were afraid to steal from him. There were the usual unfortunate confrontations, but Cook, for the most part, managed to keep the situation and his own temper under control.

The expedition continued north at the beginning of February. Cook gradually began to take his ships to the northeast, and in early March he sighted New Albion—present-day Oregon. Cook planned to follow this coastline northward until he reached the Bering Strait, the narrow stretch of water separating Asia and North America near the Arctic Circle. At that time, the coasts of Canada and Alaska were virtually unknown to Europeans, and thus Cook began to chart them with his customary precision and accuracy. Describing the coast in his journal, Cook wrote that "the land consists of high hills and deep vallies, for the most part clothed with large timber, such as Spruce fir and white Cedar. The more inland mountains were covered with snow."

Cook found a good harbor in Nootka Sound, located on the seaward side of present-day Vancouver Island. Many Indians inhabited this bay region, and without hesitation they came out to the ships in their canoes and began to trade their furs with the visitors. The Nootka Indians were nothing like the Polynesians, and at first the white men reacted to them with distaste. Compared to the Polynesians, the Nootka seemed primitive, strange looking, and dirty, and their language had a harsh, almost savage quality. But as their stay in Nootka Sound lengthened, the visitors grew quite comfortable with the Nootka, who were proud but courteous, predictable but intelligent, and good-natured unless provoked. They were also independent and self-sufficient, and had no fear of the white

A family of Nootka Indians in a communal house near Nootka Sound, located on the west coast of Vancouver Island and visited by Cook's expedition in April 1778. The Nootka, Cook wrote, "were a docile, courteous, good-natured people," but "when displeased, they are exceedingly violent."

men or their weapons; therefore, the white men treated them as equals and there was a mutual respect. Soon, members of the expedition had open invitations to the Nootka villages. The expedition's stay in Nootka Sound turned out to be one of their most pleasant, and the kind of ugly incidents that plagued the explorers' interaction with the Polynesians were conspicuously absent.

After a month in Nootka Sound, where the abundant timber of the region was used to repair the *Resolution*'s masts, the ships continued up the coast, and the search for the Northwest Passage began in earnest. If a passage did indeed exist, Cook was as determined to find it as he

While skirting the edges of the Arctic ice pack in August 1778, Cook's men caught their first sight of the fearsome polar bear, which they referred to as the "white bear." The Nootka and other native inhabitants of the Arctic region hunted the bear for its thick, water-repellent pelt.

had been determined to prove that no giant landmass existed in the South Pacific. For seven arduous months the *Resolution*, followed by the *Discovery*, inched northward along the coast of present-day British Columbia and Alaska, sailing into any inlet or bay or sound that might possibly be the entrance to the Northwest Passage. But always they were forced to turn back, finding only dead ends. Cook spent two weeks surveying one large indentation in the coast, known today as Cook Inlet, following it inland only to see the rocky, snowcapped mountains close in upon the ships and force him to turn around. Following the Alaska Peninsula and the Aleutian Islands to the west, the ships found a passage through to the Bering Sea in June.

Cook continued up the Alaskan coast through July, reaching its westernmost point, Cape Prince of Wales, at the end of the month. On August 3, the *Resolution* and the *Adventure* sailed through the Bering Strait; visible to starboard was North America, to port, mainland Asia. After stopping briefly on the desolate Asian coast, the ships sailed out of the Bering Strait into the Arctic Sea. Cook pushed northward for six more days until he encountered a sight that veterans of his Antarctic voyages recognized immediately—an impenetrable wall of ice. Cook had gone as far north as he could. The ships were battered, his men were worn out, and the Arctic winter would soon close in on them. He decided to return to Hawaii for the winter, to the delight of all hands. In the spring they would come north again and continue the search for the Northwest Passage.

Members of a hunting party from the Resolution *take aim at a herd of walrus. At that time the animals were known as sea horses, even though, as Cook noted, "they have not the least resemblance of a horse. It is certainly more like a cow than a horse; but this likeness consists in nothing but the snout. In short, it is an animal like a seal, but incomparably larger."*

"We Have Lost Our Father!"

On the final day of November 1778 the *Resolution* and the *Discovery* reached the island of Hawaii. They sailed along its northeastern and southeastern coasts for a tiresome six weeks, searching for a calm harbor between the booming waves and the rocky, jagged shoreline. The Hawaiians paddled their canoes out to the ships periodically to trade with the visitors. Finally, in mid-January 1779, Cook found a suitable bay and the ships dropped anchor there. It was called Kealakekua Bay.

Relations between the visitors and the islanders were complex and problematic, hinging on cultural misapprehension rather than understanding. Most of the Hawaiian people seemed to think that Cook was a god and they treated him with great deference. The Hawaiian chiefs seemed to share this view, but they also resented Cook's presence and were soon asking him pointedly how long he planned to stay. Cook sensed some hostility, and he decided it would be best to leave as soon as possible. The ships sailed out of Kealakekua Bay in early February 1779. They had not gone far when a violent storm damaged the *Resolution*'s masts. Cook decided to return to Kealakekua Bay for repairs.

Although he had been gone for only a week, Cook returned to Hawaii to find that he was no longer a god. Either he had done something just before he left that disillusioned the Hawaiians, or the chiefs, unhappy to see the ships returning, had convinced the people that Cook

A man of the Sandwich Islands (Hawaiian Islands) in ceremonial headdress. After spending the summer months of 1778 searching for the Northwest Passage along the west coast of North America, Cook returned to Hawaii, where he hoped the expedition might comfortably pass the winter. But instead of a safe harbor, Cook found death.

was a mere mortal. Whatever the reason, Cook and his
companions were now regarded with unconcealed resentment and even animosity. There was a rash of petty theft
and harassment, culminating in the disappearance of one
of the *Discovery*'s longboats. Cook decided that he could
not let this go. He sent a number of marines and sailors
to search the bay for the missing longboat while he went
ashore with a party of marines, intending to take one of
the chiefs prisoner until the boat was returned.

As Cook and several marines led their hostage down the beach a large crowd of Hawaiians gathered. The mood of the crowd was ugly; many of them were gathering stones and some were armed with spears, clubs, and daggers. As Cook and his men backed away from the crowd into the water, stones were thrown, shots were fired, and before they could reload or retreat the Hawaiians fell on them. Cook and four of his companions were stabbed and clubbed to death in the shallows. The other marines made

Hawaiians come out to greet Cook upon his return to Kealakekua Bay. The islanders were as comfortable in the ocean—swimming or sailing—as they were on land. "It was very common," Cook wrote, "to see women with infants at the breast . . . leap overboard, and without endangering their little ones, swim to the shore through a sea that looked dreadful."

it back out to the ships, although some of them were badly wounded.

It was a shockingly brutal and sudden end for Cook, and shock was the prevailing reaction on the *Resolution* and the *Discovery* for several hours. All hands gathered on deck and stared in silence at the now deserted beach, unable to comprehend the magnitude of the event. Finally, as darkness fell, stunned disbelief gave way to anguish and horror. On the island, the Hawaiians could hear the sounds of grief drifting in from the ships anchored in the bay. One sailor was heard to cry, "We have lost our father!"

That sorrowful comment probably best represents the relationship between Cook and his men and the impact of his death on them. Cook was indeed a father figure to his crews; stern yet fair, feared yet loved, exacting yet forgiving. His concern for the well-being of his men was nothing less than fatherly; he would protect them from disease, for example, even if he had to punish them in order to do so. (Many historians believe that his greatest achievement was not in the area of navigation, seamanship, or discovery, but rather in the improvements he pioneered in naval medicine, particularly regarding the problem of scurvy. No other mariner, before or since, has done so much to improve the lot of the common sailor.) Cook would never subject his crew to risks or hardships he was not willing to undertake himself. His men, for their part, literally followed him anywhere; they might have grumbled and complained sometimes, but they always followed, for they all seemed to agree that James Cook was a great man—perhaps the greatest sea captain ever.

And indeed he probably was. The accomplishments of James Cook were staggering. As an explorer of the world's oceans and as a navigator, he simply has no equal. In 10 years, Cook plied the earth's waters from the Antarctic Circle to the Arctic Circle, from Newfoundland to New Zealand, circumnavigating the planet three times in the

process. And unlike the explorers who came before him, Cook charted and mapped, with detail and precision, every nautical mile of his voyages. In this respect, Cook was the exemplary nautical explorer, the navigator who set the standard for all other navigators. It can safely be said that in his time no man knew the world as well as Captain Cook, and no other explorer had such an impact on the global map.

The *Resolution* and the *Discovery* remained in Kealakekua Bay for several days, attempting to get the remains of Cook back from the islanders and considering what kind of reprisal, if any, should be made. Some men wanted to shell the island with the ships' big guns; some wanted to

Hawaiian priests pay homage to Captain Cook in a religious ceremony shortly before his death. Many of the islanders believed that Cook was the incarnation of the god Lono, who, according to Hawaiian tradition, was to come to the islands from the ocean.

The Death of Captain Cook, *by John Webber. "Our unfortunate commander," recalled one of Cook's officers who witnessed the event, "the last time he was seen distinctly, was standing at the water's edge, and calling out to the boats to cease firing and pull in . . . . Thus fell our great and excellent commander!"*

go ashore and raze the villages; and some argued for a truce with the islanders. Negotiations were undertaken for the return of Cook's body; the islanders reported that he had been dismembered and his parts scattered about the island. A troop of marines then went ashore and ran amok, burning villages and decapitating Hawaiians. Finally, a piece of Cook's head and some of his bones, as well as his gun, were brought out to the *Resolution.* A naval funeral ceremony was held at sunset; Cook's remains were burned and the ashes released to the sea. Then, with the cannons booming a final hail and farewell to their captain, the two ships sailed out of Kealakekua Bay. They arrived at London in October 1780.

Further Reading

Badger, G. M. *Captain Cook: Navigator and Scientist*. London: Hurst, 1970.

Beaglehole, J. C. *The Life of James Cook*. Stanford: Stanford University Press, 1974.

Blackwood, Alan. *Captain Cook*. New York: Watts, 1987.

Brown, Warren. *The Search for the Northwest Passage*. New York: Chelsea House, 1991.

Cameron, Ian. *Lost Paradise: The Exploration of the Pacific*. Topsfield, MA: Salem House, 1987.

Chickering, William H. *Within the Sound of These Waves: The Story of the Kings of Hawaii Island*. Westport, CT: Greenwood Press, 1971.

Cook, James. *Captain Cook: Voyages of Discovery*. London: Alan Sutton, 1984.

Day, Grove D. *Captain Cook*. Honolulu: Hogarth, 1977.

Elliot, John, and Richard Pickersgill. *Captain Cook's Second Voyage: The Journals of Lieutenants Elliot and Pickersgill*. Wolfeboro, NH: Longwood Press, 1984.

Fisher, Robin, and Hugh Johnston. *Captain James Cook and His Times*. Seattle: University of Washington Press, 1979.

Forster, George. *A Voyage Around the World in H.M.S. Resolution*. Wolfeboro, NH: Longwood Press, 1986.

Holmes, Maurice. *Captain James Cook*. Philadelphia: Franklin, 1969.

Kennedy, Gavin. *The Death of Captain Cook*. Wolfeboro, NH: Longwood Press, 1987.

Sylvester, David W. *Captain Cook and the Pacific Reeves.* White Plains, NY: Longman, 1971.

Vaughn, Thomas, and C. M. Murray-Oliver. *Captain Cook, R.N.: The Resolute Mariner.* Portland: Oregon Historical Society, 1976.

Withey, Lynne. *Voyages of Discovery: Captain Cook and the Exploration of the Pacific.* New York: Morrow, 1987.

Wolfe, Cheri. *Lt. Charles Wilkes and the Great U.S. Exploring Expedition.* New York: Chelsea House, 1991.

Zimmerman, Heinrich. *The Third Voyage of Captain Cook.* Fairfield, WA: Ye Galleon, 1988.

Chronology

Entries in roman type refer to events directly related to exploration and Cook's life; entries in italics refer to important historical and cultural events of the era.

1522	Spanish expedition begun under the command of Ferdinand Magellan concludes the first circumnavigation of the globe, thereby giving Europe its first glimpse of the extent of the Pacific Ocean
1642	Dutch mariner Abel Tasman discovers Tasmania and New Zealand
1660	*Royal Society formed in London for the purpose of promoting scientific discussion*
Oct. 27, 1728	James Cook born in Marton-in-Cleveland, North Yorkshire, England
1746	Begins a nine-year apprenticeship under coal-shippers Henry and John Walker
1755	Joins Royal Navy
1756	*French and Indian War begins for control of North American colonies*
1759	Cook takes part in British siege of Quebec
1763	*Peace of Paris ends the French and Indian War*
1767–68	British mariner Samuel Wallis becomes European discoverer of Tahiti; followed there a year later by French explorer Louis-Antoine de Bougainville, whose enchanted reports give rise to the Enlightenment concepts of the noble savage and the island paradise
1768	The Royal Society convinces the English Admiralty to undertake a scientific expedition to the South Pacific; Cook appointed to lead the expedition; expedition embarks for Tahiti in August

1769	*Endeavor* rounds Cape Horn in January; reaches Tahiti in April; transit of Venus observed in June; expedition reaches New Zealand in October
1770	*Endeavor* reaches Botany Bay, on Australia's southeast coast, in April; sails northward to chart the coastline; Cook almost wrecks the *Endeavor* on the Great Barrier Reef; 33 crew members die of dysentery and malaria contracted in Dutch Indonesia
1771	*Endeavor* reaches England in July; Cook receives permission from the Admiralty to conduct a second voyage; two ships, the *Resolution* and the *Adventure*, are purchased for the expedition
July 1772	*Resolution* and *Adventure* set sail from Plymouth
1773	Cook's expedition becomes the first to cross the Antarctic Circle
1774	Cook, in the *Resolution*, reaches the lowest latitude yet recorded; the expedition explores Easter Island, the Marquesas, the Society Islands, New Hebrides, and New Caledonia
July 1775	Cook and the *Resolution* return to England, where he learns that 10 members of the *Adventure*'s crew were devoured by cannibals in New Zealand
1776	Offered command of an expedition to search for the Northwest Passage; the *Resolution* and the *Discovery* set sail from Plymouth in July, the same month that *Britain's American colonies declare their independence*
1777	Expedition visits New Zealand, Tonga, and the Society Islands
1778	Cook discovers the Hawaiian Islands in January, reaches the coast of Oregon in March, and charts the Alaskan and Canadian coastline; returns to Hawaii
Feb. 1779	Cook and four crewmen killed by Hawaiians

Index